A Duck - but tall in the water . . .

by

Lesley Wells

This book is written for my family, both the one I was born into and the one I've helped build; and for all those wonderful friends who have helped us along the way. It's dedicated to my incredible husband Michael who has been there for me every step of the way, and kept me laughing most of the time. But above all it's in gratitude to a wonderful God who has shown us that he keeps his promises.

Contents

Why a Tall Duck?

I was travelling one summer morning on a commuter train from Hastings to London. The carriage was open style with every seat taken. Most people were engrossed in a book or newspaper, or just gazing at the view from the window. Sitting quietly was a three-or-four-year-old little girl, on her mother's lap busily filling in her colouring book of birds. We knew it was bird pictures since earlier her mother had read her the text under each picture and we all enjoyed the descriptions. Suddenly this little one, who had been amazingly quiet, started to shout with great excitement "Look Mummy, look it's a . . . erm, erm - duck! But tall in the water!"

As one, every other occupant of the carriage swiftly lowered their reading material, and thirty or so pairs of eyes swivelled towards the window the little girl was pointing at. To our delight, there, at the side of a pond, stood a splendid heron in all its glory. This was followed by exchanges of smiles and the soft laughter that accompanies something precious.

I remember thinking, as we continued our journey towards the smoke, 'what a wonderful description, that's just what I am - just a duck, but one that feels tall in the water. If I ever get around to writing my life's story - that will be the title.' Just sometimes the odd thoughts we had long ago are remembered and actually come to pass!

By Way of Introduction

I grew up knowing I was adopted, but it was a long time before I started to understand the circumstances; it was even longer before I was able to comprehend just how odd my childhood was. Now in my seventh decade I find, in looking back, that I'm just amazed that I even survived, and even more amazed at what a wonderful adult life I have lived despite the bumpy start. But let's start the story by putting adoption into perspective in a way it seldom is, even today - from the perspective of the child.

In the long-running television series *Long Lost Family* host, Nicky Campbell, revealed how he felt like an impostor in his own life'. Like many of the people who feature in this programme he too was adopted; and although he had a happy childhood and was very close to his adoptive parents, he admitted to often feeling 'just not normal'.

Some years ago I came across the book The Primal Wound: *Understanding the adopted child* by Nancy Verrier. GoodReads describes it as:

> *. . . a book that is revolutionising the way we think about adoption. In its application of information about pre- and perinatal psychology, attachment, bonding, and loss, it clarifies the effects of separation from the birth mother on adopted children. In addition, it gives those children, whose pain has long been unacknowledged or misunderstood, validation for their feelings, as well as explanations for their behaviour.*

I certainly found it revolutionised my thinking and made me realise how blessed Michael and I have been to have the strong bonds we have with our children.

Verrier explains:

> Adoption, then, has been seen as the best solution to three problems: a biological mother who cannot, will not or is discouraged from taking care of her infant; the child who is then relinquished; the infertile couple who want a child. The fantasy has been that the joining together of the latter two entities would produce a happy solution for everyone. The reality, however, has often been less than ideal. Despite the continuity of relationship which adoption provides, many adopted children experience themselves as unwanted, are unable to trust the permanency of the adoptive relationship and often demonstrate emotional disturbances and behavioural problems.
>
> The statistics are staggering. Although adoptees make up only 2 to 3 percent of the population, statistics consistently indicate that 30 to 40 percent of those children found in special schools, juvenile hall and residential treatment centres are adopted. Adopted children have a higher incidence of juvenile delinquency, sexual promiscuity and running away from home than their non-adopted peers. They also have more difficulty in school, both academically and socially. What is it which places these children at a higher psychological risk than the general population?

I suppose the simple answer to that is the question I often put to myself as a child "well if your own mother didn't want you, why would anyone else?" But of course there is much more to it than just the pain of rejection.

I've recently watched a video of a young Chinese woman who was adopted by a British couple when she was two; this would have been sometime in the late 1980s to early 90s. Jinling has expressed through the medium of poetry what it feels like to not know where you come from and to always feel that you don't fit in. She is loved by and loves her adoptive parents but is bravely saying adoption isn't a simple solution to a problem and is always painful since you wish it had never had to happen. In her own words:

> Adoption is not simple, yet most people have a superficial view of what adoption means. As I grew up, the narrative was controlled by only one side of the adoption process and I realised that there were so many instances of adoption being portrayed through the media, solely focusing on the experience for adoptive parents. It seemed strange to me that there was so little focus on adopted children and their perspectives. It was as if it never occurred to anyone to ask them. Further, adoptees that spoke out with anything other than gratitude were ostracised by a society that only sees the value of adoption without recognising the trauma. (Jinling Wu - BBC website 10/03/21)

Despite the rather depressing context to my childhood and teen years they should be regarded as merely background scenery - they do not define me or my story. Definitely not. I've always loved life and feel that I've lived a great deal of it on a rollercoaster; which is fine by me since being scared half to death on terrifying fairground rides is my idea of a grand way to spend a day.

So pack some tissues and a few snacks and join me on the ride of my lifetime.

Early Memories

It was a beautiful sunny day and so all our cots were out on one of the lawns, laid out in three or four straight rows military style, so that we would benefit from the fresh air and sunshine. Children were put out to air as often as possible in those days. I remember looking up and down my row seeing each cot occupied by a baby or toddler dressed in romper suit and sun hat and with one soft toy to keep them company. I remember our sunny nap time being interrupted by the arrival of a man, dressed all in grey, accompanied by two white clad figures. The party arrived at the first cot in my row and the occupant was scooped up by one of the angels. Suddenly, Grey Man appeared to hit the baby's leg and our tranquillity was shattered by the high-pitched screams of the innocent victim.

All of us clutched hold of our cot sides and tried to see what had caused this outrage. We could see one of the angels in white returning the baby to its cot and the screams were now subsiding into wails. Just as we thought it was all over and were plonking back down on our well-padded bottoms another ruckus began, this time the victim was older and was roaring his indignation. I stayed standing this time and watched the party progress slowly towards my own cot. Years later, when I learned the meaning of the word inexorable, I remembered that day and realised, I already knew what it meant.

All too quickly they arrived at my cot and I was lifted into the arms of an angel, before I had time to enjoy the experience the grey man did something to my leg that caused me to be as hurt, angry and terrified as those who had gone before me, and who were still rubbing their legs. I suppose had they explained what inoculation meant we would all have been too young to have known or cared; but I still remember the shock, and like a great many people of my generation I bear the physical scar to this day.

Memory is a haphazard thing and looking back over the years little flashes of memory illustrate the past. Inevitably any memory comes with its own built-in question; is that really how it happened? But these are my memories and I present them as the images that helped shape me and create the individual that I am.

****

So let's start right at the beginning. I was born on Tuesday the eleventh of April 1950 to Doris and James Magee and given the names of Dorothy Rosanna.

I was not an only child, I had an older brother, Leonard Roberts Magee, born in the post war baby boom of 1947, and James, born posthumously, some eleven months younger than myself. Our father who had served as a regular soldier both before and throughout the second world war had contracted tuberculosis shortly before peace was declared. Even though the drug streptomycin had already been isolated in the United States some three years later, clinical trials had not yet started; he died in 1951.

I must have been less than a year old but this particularly vivid memory has remained with me. I seem to have retained a mental 'video' of myself lying in a cot watching two adults standing close to me talking. Since I was so young I doubt that I had any understanding of what was being said, but just as we have the capacity to remember snatches of music from way back, so too, perhaps, we have the innate ability to remember a string of words until such time as our language has developed and we find the sounds turn into words and the words have meaning. In any case, I remember a man wearing what seemed like a band of white cloth around his mouth saying "Well this one's going to do well!" A fragment of recollected history that finally made sense many years later when I met my mother and recounted this memory to her. She was so shocked that she actually broke down; she remembered it too. And yes, my father had been wearing a facemask because of his tuberculosis.

Language recognition certainly is a funny thing. If I ever came home looking untidy I was told "you look like the wreck of Hesperus". On hearing that phrase your brain's search assistant probably pulled up a picture of some famous wreck. But people didn't often bother to explain things to children in those days and you were seldom encouraged to ask. So my brain just remembered that I looked like whatever that strange sounding word 'wreckofthehesperus' was. In my twenties when Michael and I were taking a school party around the Cutty Sark; as I walked around the lower deck I noticed that there was a display of paintings of famous shipwrecks, and of course one of them was the *Wreck of the Hesperus*. I've never forgotten how foolish I felt, and vowed I would always take the time to explain the strange things we say to our children.

Back to my poor mother, an only child who had been raised by elderly parents, whom she described as 'cold and distant', had spent her childhood starved of affection, and then lost the love of her life after just a few short years. To add insult to injury she was left with three very small, very dependent children, who felt equally starved of affection; and whose sole task, so she believed at the time, was to drive her insane with their endless demands for care and attention. It is reported that the only time Len stopped crying during his first eighteen months was when he was asleep. It must have been a downward spiral of sadness, frustration, and despair

Another early memory features at least one clumsy adult. We were sitting on a blanket in the sunshine when it suddenly started to rain heavily. Another of those quite startling childhood memories since I could only have been around eighteen months old on this particular occasion. Apparently it was the day after my father's funeral and some of my father's brothers and relatives had come over from Northern Ireland for the event. We had gone over to the nearby Wanstead Flats to get some fresh air when suddenly a thunderstorm came out of nowhere. My mother recalls that one of them grabbed me off the blanket and then snatched up the blanket and set off at a pace back to the house. Unfortunately he caught his foot in the blanket causing the two of us to hurtle into some brambles, this annoyance caused him to hold me far too tight as he set off again. My memory is of the physical discomfort of having the air squeezed out of me and my soft little cheek being repeatedly rubbed against a very rough and scratchy jacket. I also felt an overwhelming sense of the sadness emanating from him, and despite wanting to squawk my head off because of the discomfort and indignity of it all, I some how knew it was better just to keep quiet and put up with it.

This strong sense of empathy has stayed with me throughout the years; like others similarly blessed (or burdened) I can almost palpably feel other people's unspoken emotions at times. Sadly, only occasionally do I manage to put this to good use, and quite often I completely miss the obvious. It was only when I was in my forties that I discovered that one of my grandmother's brothers was the famous Col. Robert Blair Mayne, one of the co-founders of the SAS and colonel of the regiment throughout much of the war. He has often been described as the T. E. Lawrence of WWII and like him tragically died just a few short years after returning home. My mother remembers him being at my father's funeral so perhaps it was Great Uncle Paddy's hairy jacket I endured that day!

It was almost inevitable that our perceived goal was achieved, and our mother had what in those days would have been called 'a complete mental breakdown'. The National Society for the Protection of Cruelty to Children stepped in and the authorities took over. The three of us were together for one last time for a few months in one of the many Dr Barnardo's children's homes that abounded after the war. From the Smokey streets of Forest Gate in East London we were whisked away to St Christopher's, a Victorian mansion complete with stately grounds in the polite outskirts of leafy Tonbridge in Kent.

Children of today would never remember their first car-ride, for most it would be the trip home from the hospital where they were born, but cars were rarer in my early context. My first real memory of travelling in a car was of sharing it with three ladies in coats and hats (you were not considered a lady if you did not wear a hat in the early 1950s). There were two ladies in the front of the car, with my brothers and I squashed up in the back with the third. Despite the lack of space, I still remember us small people rattling about, no seat belts in those days. My guess is that James was about a year old, I would have been two and Len would have been five. What I was almost certainly remembering was being driven from our home after our mother had been hospitalised. It was possible that we were taken straight to Tonbridge, but more likely that we were taken to the Barnardo's 'clearing house' in Barkingside before being dispatched to Kent.

In any case I clearly remember the context we arrived at, wherever it was. We children, and one of the ladies, were kept for what seemed like hours in a waiting room. If I shut my eyes and think of that occasion I see nothing but a complex pattern of red-veined marble. I'm guessing that the waiting room was a partition of what had once been a large and gracious room or hallway; a long wooden bench stretched the length of the room against the wall, and the lady sat in a chair opposite us. While my brothers rolled about on or under the bench I stood on the bench facing the wall and gazing at the beautiful marble panel.

Tied up with the visual memory of the marble is the deeply emotional memory of pain and bewilderment that engulfed me. Ignoring the overtures of the kind lady, even though I sensed that she had no desire to be part of this either, I stood resolutely with my back to the world registering my protest.

Somehow my heart knew that this was a turning point and things would never be the same again. I was not wrong.

Despite the trauma of separation I always have fond memories of that children's home in Tonbridge. Not only was it a place where I felt safe, but I was well fed, and had lots of other children and toys to play with. We were looked after by young ladies who seemed like angels to us, perhaps it was the nurse's uniforms they wore with the large white aprons and caps. I'm convinced it was their efforts that finally encouraged me to talk, apparently I was still not talking properly at the age of three. I moved on from the caring Barnardo's staff speaking with what might be called a refined Surrey accent which I never lost. This was something of a stark contrast to the accents I was surrounded with, both before, and after that time.

My general impression of this place was the contrast of scale. The grounds were vast, as were the rooms and corridors, yet the chairs, basins and baths and other furniture were all the perfect size to fit us children. I always carried with me a memory of an absolutely giant rocking horse, from which if you fell would have meant certain death. You can imagine my disappointment when on a visit to St Christopher's some years later I discovered that the rocking horse, that had clearly been loved over the years, was just a standard size; and the huge marble pillars did not reach to the sky as I had remembered either. Sometimes it's best not to try to go back in time!

Another memory from St Christopher's, which has a dream-like quality about it, involved a chair and a door. There were a group us left alone in the big playroom. I imagine it was rare for us to be left without adult supervision, but it had to happen sometimes. I can remember the huge door being shut on us, and the look of indignation that passed around, the unspoken but general consensus of "Well, that's not right!"

I may not have been speaking at the time, but I've always been quick on the uptake. The others stood around watching; I'd like to say with awe, but I can't be certain, as I somehow managed to drag a full-sized chair across the room and stood it next to the door, and then proceeded to ascend its north face. You have to remember that I was less than three feet tall and this was Victorian manor house scale, so it was no mean feat. I knew that all I had to do was reach up for the big handle thingy and the door would then magically swing open, granting us our freedom; and I would be the hero of the day. I was just at the point of reaching for the handle when I stopped in amazement, since the magic had begun early.

The door handle was moving downwards all of its own accord. What I hadn't learned at that stage of things is that, generally speaking, doors are designed to open inwards into a room and not outwards. As I stood mesmerised the door suddenly flew straight towards me. I saw the chair tip away from under my feet at the exact same moment the door slammed into me. Thus began my first experience of flying, more in the style of Icarus than that of piloting a Piper Comanche 250. Without ever having met Newton I was able to fully appreciate the functions of inertia, maximum velocity, followed by zero velocity and then the amazing effects of gravity. That last phase is impressed in my mind as an image of the floor, that had once been so far below, came up, very fast, to meet my face. Strangely I can't recall anything more of that particular incident; and unaccountably it isn't mentioned in my records either.

Inevitably it is difficult trying to piece together the events of those far off years, both my brothers and I were far too young to ever have been told the official story, and although records from those times are available they are quite sparse.

But what is a matter of public record is that my brother Len, aged six, was transported to Australia. Not as a condemned prisoner, but as a hopeful and naïve child migrant, leaving me languishing in dreary England facing a very uncertain future.

Torn Asunder

My brother Len's story has been well rehearsed and even published in book form, *Coming Home* by Len Magee (with Chris Spencer); and although this is essentially my story, it might appear churlish to airbrush him out. So he gets his own chapter.

It appears that once my brothers had been returned to my mother's care two 'nice ladies' turned up on her doorstep and offered to take Len off her hands. She jumped at the opportunity, since maternal instincts were just not something poor Doris had come readily supplied with. It appears that she was one of those rare people who totally lack any sort of altruistic parental instincts, she found no joy in being with her children, generally regarding them as an unbearable burden. Lacking that parental affection gene she apparently was able to make the decision to let go of each of us, one by one. In the end my poor mother had six children and failed to keep any of us with her for more than a couple of years.

The pair of nice ladies were, what in those days might well have been called 'Do-gooders' from an organisation called The Fairbridge Society. The Fairbridge Society was established in 1909 by Kingsley Fairbridge who set-up a charity to offer opportunities for children and young people from the UK, primarily in Australia and Canada. This is an extract from a report in the Guardian in 2017:

More than 130,000 children were sent to a "better life" in former colonies, mainly Australia and Canada, from the 1920s to 1970s under the child migrant programme.

The children, aged between three and fourteen, were almost invariably from deprived backgrounds and already in some form of social or charitable care. It was believed, they would lead happier lives.

Charities such as Barnardo's and the Fairbridge Society, the Anglican and Catholic churches and local authorities helped with the organisation of the emigration.

Once there, the children were often told they were orphans to better facilitate their fresh start. The parents – many of them single mothers forced to give up their child for adoption because of poverty or social stigma – believed this was giving them best chance in life, though often did not have details of where their offspring were sent to.

The reality, for some of those children, was a childhood of servitude and hard labour at foster homes: on remote farms, at state-run orphanages and church-run institutions. They were often separated from siblings. Some were subjected to physical and sexual abuse.

In 2010, the then prime minister, Gordon Brown, issued an official apology, expressing regret for the "misguided" programme, and telling the Commons: "To all those former child migrants and their families . . . we are truly sorry. They were let down."

"We are sorry they were allowed to be sent away at the time when they were most vulnerable. We are sorry that instead of caring for them, this country turned its back".

The last children sailed in 1967. But it is only recently, as their stories have been told, that details of the abuse, and the official sanction which made it possible, has become public. The Australian government issued an apology in 2009 for the cruelty shown to child migrants. There were two aims to the child migrant programme: to ease the burden on UK orphanages; and to boost the populations of the colonies.

It was not until the early 1980s that Nottingham social worker Margaret Humphreys found out that there were former migrants in Australia who were just realising they might have living relatives in the UK. They had been told they were orphans. She has since dedicated her work to reuniting lost children with their families.

Allegations about the Fairbridge homes emerged after David Hill, a child migrant sent to the Fairbridge farm at Molong – who became chairman and managing director of the Australian Broadcasting Corporation, got together with other child migrants and highlighted the abuse in his 2007 book *The Forgotten Children* along with the Australian Broadcasting Corporation's 2009 documentary of the same name.

David Hill ended up being a resident at the same farm school where Len spent his childhood and teenage years, they remain in contact and are good friends.

In some ways I can see why this social engineering on a grand scale took place. More often than not the people and organisations involved with these mass migrations truly had the welfare of the children as a top priority. Undoubtedly though, a few who worked for the Fairbridge Society and similar organisations as house parents in the farms and homes saw this a golden opportunity to dominate and control children and as a means of gaining some power in an otherwise failed life. While others had far more sinister plans in mind and knew that 'in the back of nowhere', amongst children who belonged to no-one, their cruelty and abuse of innocent victims would go completely undetected. And they were right.

Back in the UK the child welfare organisations still clung to the conservative squirearchy view that the children of poor parents who weren't coping were better off starting a 'new life'. It didn't enter their thinking that the best recourse would be to spend time and money working with the worn-out, abandoned, or widowed parent in order to keep a family together. That sort of thinking was a long way off. However, it was the ethos of the time and, to a certain extent, I can understand it. What I find impossible to understand is why the authorities kept sending children to these places many years after the stories of brutality and molestation had started to make their way back to the homeland. As the Guardian reported:

> In 1956, three British officials visited Australia on a fact-finding mission to inspect 26 institutions which took child migrants, and delivered back a fairly critical report, identifying issues such as lack of expertise in childcare, and concerns of the remote rural locations. The report, however, made no mention of sexual or physical abuse. And the child migration continued.

What they forgot to mention was that all of the institutions were notified, weeks in advance, of the impending visit; I dread to think what they might have found if they had turned up on a surprise inspection. Just as damaging, in a different kind of way was the lack of care and emotional input these children experienced. As Len once wrote in an article:

> *For the next six years I lived with fourteen other boys in a sparse wooden cottage with a cottage mother who I'm sure was the inspiration behind the cartoon character Cruella Deville. She successfully managed to suffocate and crush our little spirits before they had a chance to even surface. We were beaten, intimidated, and filled with such fear that our lives would never be normal again!*

> *Somehow I found some solace in winning a scholarship to Hurlstone Agricultural High School in Sydney where, apart from my holidays back working on the Farm, I spent three years. Eventually when I left Fairbridge at the age of 17, I was insecure, unskilled, and socially inept. I was unable to open a bank account or even use a telephone. The lack of loving nurture and parental support had taken a heavy toll over those early formative years!*

I remember seeing Len and David Hill on a television interview, when the extent of the cruelty to these children was finally being revealed and enquiries were starting; how I wept when I heard Len say "At times I felt so alone and broken that I would just curl up into a foetal position and beg to die."

Again, hindsight is a wonderful thing, and I have no doubt of the good intentions of most of the people concerned, but I am amazed and saddened by the lying and duplicity that was served to both children and parents by those who knew better. Time and time again the system was described as providing new and wonderful homes for Britain's orphans. I saw an interview with someone who had been the matron of the Barkingside home that acted as a clearinghouse for countless children about to enter the migration system. She recalled that she had seen many hundreds of children come and go over the years and probably less than twenty were genuine orphans. All the rest were simply the product of social engineering by a stratum of society that believed that being poor equated with being not very bright and probably feckless, and therefore it was the better thing just to relieve these struggling parents of their offspring and let both children and adults spend the rest of their lives wondering what happened to the people they were supposed to be with.

Telling the children they were orphans was part of the lie, possibly aimed at numbing the pain, and undoubtedly preferable to being told, as many children were "well you just weren't wanted"! For the vast majority of children this would have simply been untrue, and for the few where it might have been - that would certainly have been the time to conceal the truth!

So many of the parents were told that it was just for a short time, and yet others, like my mother, were completely duped. When the 'nice ladies' saw how interested my mother was in the Fairbridge Scheme they came back for more visits and repeatedly told her that the scheme was keen on reuniting families and that once little Lennie was settled in his new home she would be encouraged to go over to Australia with her other children and settle down and have a nice life there.

Whether my mother would have signed the papers if she hadn't been spun that story is hard to say, but one thing is certain, there wasn't an ounce of truth in it. Yes, some families did manage to get themselves over to Australia or Canada to catch up with their missing children, but they did so by their own efforts. There are no records of any of the organisations involved paying for families to migrate, with or after their children. In her naivete, my mother spent many years dreaming of a new life in Australia. Amazingly she did emigrate to Australia when she was in her sixties and died there a few years ago, but I don't think she ever found it matched up to her dreams. Far from going to find her missing son, she had to wait for him to find her.

Perhaps we can leave this sad narrative with one final picture of a six-year-old boy, feeling abandoned on the eve of a lonely voyage to the other side of the world, having said goodbye to his mother. "All I can remember of that visit," he later wrote, "is watching her walk away down the drive, her bright red coat a mass of poppies swaying in the breeze, and me knowing instinctively that I never would see her again."

Barnardo's

As mentioned I spent a few years, on and off, at St Christopher's Dr Barnardo's Children's Home and have only very fond memories of my time there.

When our daughter, Carolyn, was awarded her master's degree in 2009 it was presented to her by Dr Barnardo, the great great-grandson of the original Dr Barnardo. Not only did Carolyn know him but Michael had met him and his family a few times when he preached at their church. I was finally privileged to meet the man whose ancestor had instigated the creation of proper children's home, as opposed to the workhouses and orphanages of the past, that provided places of safety and care for myself and my brothers and so many like us.

To me, St Christopher's was a place of peace and security and was full of people who actually seemed to care about us. Years later, when I had finally met my mother again and had a baby of my own, I remember her watching me as I was singing and chatting to Carolyn as I was changing her. I was astounded when she asked "why do you bother with all that, she can't understand a word you're saying, she's too young?" At that point I hadn't started down my route to education but even I knew that babies learn to talk by being talked to. Perhaps that, combined with the break-up of our family, explains why I didn't really start talking until I was almost three. I vaguely remembered an incident in Barnardo's, and later read the official notes on it, where I was put to share a room with a little Greek Cypriot boy, about my age, who had only just arrived and didn't speak a word of English.

Apparently we fell out and ended up having a much more serious fight than most toddlers can manage, which culminated with him biting me hard on the cheek. When we were asked what we were fighting about, neither of us was actually in a position to explain – so I'm still not sure why I ended up with a scar on my cheek!

social engineering

Noun [u]

>   the artificial controlling or changing of how a society develops:
>   • The country has a long history of attempting social engineering through laws and regulations that many people would consider intrusive
>   • any act that influences a person to take an action that may or may not be in their best interests

The term is used today more in the context of information technology, but in the times I'm talking about it would only have been used as an anthropological or sociological term.

Getting to know my mother as an adult I asked her how she came to allow my brother Len to be sent to Australia. She was never really capable of explaining the past in any great detail, partly I think because of her lack of education, but also, more likely perhaps, because her memories were too painful; she understandably wanted the past to be 'another country'. But she did say that trying to raise three children under four completely on her own, she had no relatives around, and having to work since she couldn't manage on the small pension the army provided, was just too much for her. At the stage when she was just beginning to recover from her breakdown, she had her two boys, Len and James, back home with her. Apparently I was left at St Christopher's on my own, being the middle child perhaps that seems an odd way of doing a 'phased return'. I have a suspicion it may have been her choice and that she was already starting to see me as the most likely to be adopted, since she did once say, years later, "well I never really liked girls". Thanks Mum!

****

Jumping to the distant future, one amazing story about our mother that Len and I both recall with a certain amount of incredulity, took place a few years after our mother had emigrated to Australia in the early 90s. Our younger brother James had also emigrated and Heather, Len's wife, had quite a few members of her family now living there too, including her parents. One Christmas a family gathering was going on to which our mother and James were invited. Heather's mother didn't know our mother very well and I'm sure was trying to make friendly conversation when, in the middle of the meal, she exclaimed "imagine, having had five children!" "No, six" said Heather. "What?" said a shocked James "there's Len, Lesley, me and the twins - who's the sixth?". "Ah" said our mother "I haven't told you about your younger sister yet have I?" Apparently she had told everyone else but forgotten to mention it to James. These things do slip your mind sometimes don't they!

The In-between Years

While Len was being packed up and shipped off to Australia I was still in care at St Christopher's. I don't remember my mother visiting after the boys returned home. In my records it recounts how I had my third birthday there, and since no cards or presents had arrived, the nurses got together and bought me a lovely little teddy bear - small and round, just like me! In fact, he was such a splendid fellow that he was the only item that I bought with me from my childhood; indeed, Little Ted became much loved by our son as a toddler, and still remains in his possession. When I cast my mind back I can see my dear father-in-law, patiently sewing new tartan paws on Little Ted to replace the worn-out leather ones, carefully watched by his concerned grandchildren.

Quite naturally it was always the hope and expectation of Barnardo's and other children's home that the children in their care would either return to their former homes or find new ones. In those busy years of the early fifties, in the fading days of the empire, it must have been quite hard work trying to sort out so many families who had been torn asunder by the war. So many parents lost and even where they survived, so many relationships could not withstand the changes and so more bereavement followed. It was not surprising that St Christopher's started to send me for short stays with prospective foster parents. I have a few vague memories of this, none particularly worrying, but I do remember always being glad when I arrived back 'home' at St Christopher's. Eventually I started to go for regular visits with a couple who lived in Redhill in Surrey, Tom and Muriel Peters, and then on a more permanent basis with the expectation of adoption. (See *Appendix* for Barnardo's report on this)

I remember the very first time I went to their home, a small, terraced house in a side street, which they shared with Muriel's elderly mother, Lydia; the only grandparent I ever knew and someone that I grew to love. As we went in the front door their large black and tan terrier dog came running down the corridor to greet us. I say large, I have no idea how big it really was but I do know it's face was level with mine and when it started licking my face I was convinced it was trying to eat me. It was quite likely the first dog I had come into close contact with and I don't think a ravening lion would have been more frightening. Strangely, I didn't develop a fear of canines and ended up adoring most all dogs and definitely all donkeys. But it was not an auspicious start to the relationship.

It was a long time before the memories of St Christopher's began to fade and I continued to feel homesick for years. In later years, when Muriel sensed she wasn't going to win an argument except by the usual recourse to brute force, she occasionally threatened to send me back to Barnardo's. My immediate and genuine response was to rush to find a bag and start stuffing clothes in it; not surprisingly, she did not try that very often. I would not have had the words to explain it at the time but looking back I can see that I lived with a sense of oppression, caused by both the house and the foster parents. It was not their fault of course that the house seemed like a doll's house after St Christopher's. The scale of St Christopher's never bothered me, probably because the rooms my mother had lived in were part of a much bigger, and probably once much grander house, and although we probably only occupied two or three rooms, they were tall and well proportioned. Though I would have been very young when I last stood on that floor I retained a memory of a large spiral staircase, with lots of doors leading off, while on the ground floor the staircase ended with a black and white chequer-board floor, where the pram was stored. Years later my mother confirmed my memory of my early home, right down to the harlequin tiles.

Consequently moving into a tiny house with people I didn't really know, and with no other children about, was quite traumatic for a sensitive little soul like me. Yes, let me at this early stage confess to being a petal; I'd really rather not be, and I have toughened up somewhat, but that is the fact of the matter. Gradually both the dog and the Granny won me over, but with the Peter's it never happened. How much of this failed relationship can be laid at the feet of a mere child, and a damaged one at that, is hard to say; and I certainly must have been a difficult child to handle. But I think that ability to read people, which I've always had, allowed me to sense that they were not genuine. The dog and the Granny were, but they were not. What do I mean by that? Well as a parent and grandparent I know that having children is not only about joy and privilege, but also about sacrifice. You recognise that your job is to raise your little fledglings up to be able to take care of themselves and one day fly the nest and start their own lives. Oh the pain when you watch them launch off, and oh the joy when they come flapping back for a visit. In my view being a parent has nothing to do with what your child will do for you, but absolutely everything about what you can do for them. They did not ask to be born, and other than the usual respect and care we should show to all people, they do not actually owe us anything.

That was not the Peter's view of parenting or adopting a child. I know this, because they told me many times from the age of about eight onwards, "We took you out of the gutter, so you owe us. Your job, as soon as you're old enough, is to get a good job and start looking after us in our old age." In short, I was their insurance policy. If this surprises you let me put them into some kind of context.

Thomas had been born in Ramsgate in 1895, he fought in the first world war and lost the youngest of his three sons in the second war. I remember seeing a photo of Thomas as a small child and was amazed to see him wearing a dress, as indeed did most little boys in Victorian England before they went to school. One of his childhood jobs was to open the lodge gates of the estate on which his parents worked, to allow entrance to the visiting carriages; there were cars around but they were a rare sight indeed and a cause of great excitement. It's my belief that Thomas and his generation were the ones that lived through the most changes in the world and in society in the shortest time span. In his lifetime he went from horse and carriage being the usual form of transport to seeing men walking on the moon. Male universal suffrage had only come into being two years before he was born and he didn't see women getting the vote until he was in his thirties. The telephone was new and wonderful in his childhood and then the radio arrived in his late twenties. By the age of fifty-eight he was watching the Coronation on his own television along with much of the rest of the country. He went from watching silent films to going regularly to watching Hollywood blockbusters, with sound and colour, weekly in the local cinema. By the time he died, aged eighty, in 1975, the computer age was in its infancy.

My adopted father had trained as a printer and spent most of his working life as a linotype operator for a local newspaper. When he retired he had been in a senior role and was earning one of the highest wages a working man could earn, certainly more than many junior professionals. He had married and had three sons, but sadly that marriage ended in divorce and there was a lot of ill feeling between him and his two remaining sons who blamed him for the breakup of the marriage. Muriel was around twenty years younger than Thomas. I was once told that since they knew they would not be able to have children Muriel was adamant that they would adopt a child. Thomas made it quite clear that he had no desire to start another family anyway, and as he was beyond the age that any adoption society would consider, and on top of that a divorcee, it was not going to happen. This may appear harsh by today's standards, but in those days it was still very much frowned upon for ordinary working folk to get divorced; only film stars and politicians were allowed to get up to those sort of shenanigans!

Notwithstanding they did apply to Barnardo's to adopt a child, but in the paperwork they failed to make mention of any divorce and recorded his age as some fifteen years younger than that on his birth certificate.

Thomas had two sons from his first marriage, Leslie who sadly was killed in action, and after whom I was later renamed, and Dennison. He had married and had children of his own, one of whom was called Susan, and she and I attended the same school. We knew we were related since we sometimes met up at cricket match teas and there clearly was some family thing going on, I knew that her father was somehow related to my father, but not how. Susan and I were told that we were cousins, but when we discussed this at school one lunchtime, we eventually worked out that I was Susan's aunt, and she was my niece. As you can imagine, we had enormous fun with her calling me 'auntie' even thought I was only a year older than her. That is until the adults got to hear it. I don't know if Susan was told off, but I was punished, yet again, for being nosey. That's the way things were in those day. The mores of society have changed beyond recognition in my lifetime.

Many years later, when we lived in Lewes, I was invited to attend an interview for potential local magistrates. The chairman of the panel was a man by the name of Dennison Peters. One look and I knew immediately who he was, not surprisingly he didn't remember me since I'd both grown up and changed my name. I did wonder if I should declare this, but it didn't matter as I wasn't offered the role.

By the age of five I was being fostered full-time by the Peter's and so started at the local school - except it wasn't that local, we lived on the outskirts of town and St Matthews Church of England Infant and Primary School was over two miles away on the other side of town. So why did we go for an hours walk in all weathers rather than go to the really local school which was less than a ten-minute walk away? Well I guess, like most church schools today, it had a good reputation, but the main reason was that my mother had said so. No, not Muriel, but

Doris, my mother back in Barking. The strange thing was that Doris hated anything to do the with the church and religion and would cross the road if she saw the vicar coming; but when she was signing me over to Barnardo's with the prospect of adoption and they asked her if she had any preferences regarding my upbringing, she remembers blurting out "Yes, I want her to go to a church school and church or Sunday School". In the words of the old hymn *God is working his purpose out as year succeeds to year.* The fact that I spent so much time in a church context was, I believe, a strong factor that kept me safer and less damaged than I might have been otherwise.

I remember my first day in the infant class. We were all settled around a set of tables each with a toy to play with, whilst the teacher was sorting out the register and probably hustling anxious parents away. To my delight I had before me one of those wonderful old nursery toys which was basically a thin block of wood in an 'H' shape with holes for six pegs which fitted very tightly in place and which could pass through the holes, poking out on the other side. The idea was that, using the wooden mallet supplied, you whacked the pegs as hard as you could so that they soon disappeared into the wood until just their ends were showing on the viewing side. Now here's the genius part, when, after a lot of whacking and whamming, you reached that state of affairs where you turned the whole thing over and started the joyful process all over again. Many happy hours could be spent in blissful employment with such a wonderful contraption. I am sure the person who designed that simple toy should have been awarded a Nobel Prize, but I suspect they were not.

Since I was so enthusiastically involved with my hammering I failed to notice that everyone else had gone quite, until someone nudged me and I realised the teacher was talking to me. "You know" she said "I'm a bit hard of hearing when you make that noise, can you just stop for a while and tell me your name?" Hard of hearing! Oh dear, my Nanny (as I called Lydia) was hard of hearing, in fact stone deaf, and whilst we got on like a house on fire, I had to shout all the time, which was quite hard work for someone with a naturally quiet voice. So this poor lady was hard of hearing too, well I would help her out as best as I could, "Dorothy Magee" I shouted at the top of my lungs. "Thank you" she said cringing. Later, at the end of the first term when we were making Christmas decorations she asked "Why do you always shout at me but not at anyone else?" "Because you're deaf" I responded.

"No I'm not," she said "Who told you that?" We stood frowning at each other. I have no idea what she was thinking by this point, but the little voice in my head was declaring "This is a funny world."

I think I made the most of my first few years at school, despite being mildly dyslexic - though we wouldn't have called it that then, "She won't concentrate and learn her spelling" was the usual response when I tried in vain to explain that the letters just wouldn't stay still. Despite my eventual reputation for not working hard at schoolwork, I always loved school. Later it was as much because it was a place of safety and refuge as a place of learning, and even when my learning had fallen far behind and I found myself in some sort of trouble on an almost daily basis, I still wanted to be there. It was one of my most favourite places to be, along with Sunday School,

Brownies and dance classes, in fact, I was happy to be almost anywhere but home.

For someone who loved being at school and had a curious mind and a real passion for learning, it is a shame that I was not able to really take advantage of what I was offered. It was all such a struggle, rather like continually being at odds with someone you very much love. And, talking of being at odds, my inability to concentrate could not have been helped by the situation at home. Not only did I have a constant sense of failure, that horrible little voice at the back of the mind would often taunt me with "Well if your real mummy didn't want you, then why should anyone else?" I had no answer for that. While the physical and verbal abuse that had started within the first few weeks of my being permanently fostered, did nothing to help the situation. I think I can say, hand on heart, that verbal abuse cuts more deeply and causes more pain than any amount of physical abuse.

Physical wounds heal and can be forgotten, cruel words scar for ever. I still have no idea why Muriel vented all her frustration and anger on a helpless child; but perhaps such a deeply disturbed person, as she certainly was, simply has no control over themselves. But just as, seemingly sensible and kind people chose to ignore the stories coming back about the migrant children in Australia and Canada, so the ethos of most people in those days was to simply mind your own business - and you never interfered in other people's lives.

We had an elderly widowed neighbour called Mrs Doyle. Slight aside here; Mrs Doyle had an only son called Charles who trained as a hairdresser and went gadding off to America where he ended up becoming 'Chuck' and working in the Hollywood studios. Once, when he came home for a rare visit to his elderly mother, remembering the little girl next door he brought me an autograph album. It was packed full of the signatures of just about all the Hollywood greats of the time: James Stewart, Frank Sinatra, Elizabeth Taylor, Marilyn Monroe, Perry Como as well as many others I cannot recall. Most of the names didn't mean anything to me at the time although I started to recognise some of them as I grew older. On the day I left school at sixteen, as we did in those days, I wanted an autograph book to remember my friends by. Rather than allow me to buy a new autograph album, I was told to take the American one and use the empty gaps. Not surprisingly the book fell apart and eventually got thrown away. Every time I watch The Antiques Road Show I think of that little tartan clad album and wonder what it might have been worth today.

My mother provided Mrs Doyle with a cooked lunch or supper most days since she was getting frail, they were paid for of course. But my mother's violent outbursts frightened even this salty old lady, and quite often when I went to retrieve the plates, I was sworn to secrecy and asked to throw the remains of another badly cooked meal in the bin, before returning with empty plates. I knew fairly early on that most people were afraid of my mother's violence, including my father, but somehow I never had the sense to be afraid myself. Yes I reacted in the normal way, and when I was being dragged around by my hair or being thrown against the wall or the furniture, I would be screaming at the top of my voice "Don't hit me, please don't hit me." Which usually just served to remind her that hitting was the next item on the agenda. The backdrop to all my mother's roaring rage and foul language and my screaming, was the dog barking madly and Mrs Doyle hammering on our dividing wall and shouting "Stop that, leave that child alone." Half the street must have heard the ruckus which erupted at least two or three times every week, but not one of them ever did a thing about it.

When I was seventeen, and we had left Redhill for Eastbourne, I met Mrs Doyle again when she came for a holiday. She was very frail by then and I think died a few weeks later. When I took her out for a walk in her wheelchair of course we started talking about the past. "You know" she said "it really bothered me the way your mother used to lay into you almost every day, hearing you screaming like that used to make me feel quite ill, that's why I always tried knocking on the wall, but it never did any good."

I couldn't help myself, I had to ask "But you had a phone, why didn't you ring the police, or at least contact the authorities anonymously?" "Oh" she said, quite surprised by the question "It just wasn't the sort of thing we did in those days, besides if she had found out it was me she would probably have tried to kill me as well."

On a number of occasions over the years I was quite certain that Muriel was about to kill me; when she lost her temper she became totally out of control, and being quite a large, strong woman anyway, her temper seemed to give her super-human strength. When the 'berserk' was upon her she lost all sense and caution. I saw her rip doors off kitchen cupboards and overthrow a large wooden dining table. The look of madness that overcame her was almost inhuman. I've only seen that look of madness a couple of times since, both times whilst working in Her Majesty's Prison service with serious felons.

Nanny died when I was 11 - she was in her 80s. A year earlier, during the Easter holidays and sometime around my tenth birthday, Muriel got into an argument with Lydia; they were standing in the kitchen and Muriel was at the cooker frying some food. Obviously something Lydia said really upset her since she grabbed the frying pan off the cooker, spun around and hurled it directly at her mother. This was a large iron implement, red hot from the gas ring and full of hot fat. Whether Lydia ducked, or Muriel's aim was high; I can't tell since I was in the next room reading, but the frying pan went over Lydia's head and hit the back door just behind her. One of the glass panels broke, thus perhaps stopping the missile from rebounding completely back onto the old lady, but when I rushed into the room, my Nanny was covered in food and hot fat and wailing in terror and from the pain of the burns. For once I think Muriel realised she had gone too far and fled the house. When I had got Nanny sitting down and cleaned up a bit, and whilst the dog was clearing the floor, I followed her instructions to go next door and ring her other daughter and ask for help. Fortunately Mrs Doyle made the call and I just remember her saying before she put the phone down "I told you lot that she'd bloody well kill someone one day."

It wasn't long before two cars full of relatives arrived at the door, and some very serious discussions began. So serious that, to my annoyance, I was sent next door again to be kept out of the way. When I finally returned, Thomas had arrived home from work and Muriel had also returned to brazen it out. Apparently it was all her mother's fault since she had said things to deliberately upset her! By this stage Lydia had packed a suitcase and was taken off by one of the sets of relatives to a place of safety and recovery. The police were never involved of course, and the hospital were just told it was a 'cooking accident'. Deeply upsetting thought it was, and it was months before Nanny returned, I didn't think too much of it at the time. It is only looking back as an adult that I find myself amazed that everyone concerned thought it right and proper to remove the old lady from the dangers of this mad woman, and yet it was apparently perfectly alright to leave a child, who was known to be the usual target of Muriel's temper, though I doubt if they know just how much, and who would be alone with her whilst Thomas was at work.

As I said, I was scared in some ways; but not nearly enough for my own good. Possibly I inherited some of my, then unknown, Great Uncle Paddy's hero genes, which isn't quite as wonderful as it sounds. When others are very sensibly running away from danger of any kind I find myself trying to find out what's going on and how to sort it. That might have been useful had I joined the SAS, but in 'normal' life that approach has led me into all kinds of escapades. So when, as a child, I was regularly confronted by a psychopathic bully, totally bent on owning and controlling me, I just wasn't having any of it. Had I perceived the merest glint of love in the equation I may well have capitulated, love may enable you to cope with madness and even perhaps controlling manipulation; but since I did not perceive that at all, it was my will and determination to 'be myself' that stood against Muriel's endeavours to break me. And from the first week we met, we clashed at every turn.

I remember once visiting a friend who had a budgerigar. I watched, fascinated, as it kept ferociously attacking a little toy that sat on the bottom of the cage. The lower half of the toy was a hemisphere while the top half was the head and shoulders of a clown, or some such thing. The heavily weighted and rounded lower half of the toy meant that every time the budgie whacked it with its beak, the top half would fly backwards to the floor, and then in an almost magical way, instantly right itself. It often came back so fast that it hit the hapless bird smack on the beak, which of course infuriated it even more and the whole sorry story repeated itself again and again. Whilst I was only a child of around nine or ten I somehow had the insight to see this as a somewhat ridiculous re-enactment of the relationship I had with my adopted mother. I remember standing by the birdcage crying and my friend's mother, a kindly soul, asking me what was wrong. I had no words then to explain the inexorability (it's that word again) of the situation I was in. My mother would continue to abuse and attack me since she was angry with me for not being the loving, compliant child she had ordered, which in turn would focus her wild and uncontrollable temper on me. I in turn would fight back, even in the face of certain death, which would enrage her even more. Understanding how things work is one thing, explaining it adequately to another person is quite a different matter.

What I did realise in watching the budgie boxing scenario was that moving fast usually thwarted the aggressor, and I certainly learned to move fast over the years. If I had taken up boxing I might have been quite good, assuming I could manage to reach high enough to score any points! At the time

I was never really able to fathom what it was that I did that caused Muriel so much angst. I even took to writing lists, at one stage, of what I thought might be actions or behaviours that triggered the attack mode, but it never made sense. Quite the opposite in fact, because sometimes I would be shouted at for talking too much, then half an hour later, in trouble for being silent and 'stand offish'. I was often challenged with "You think you're better than us don't you?" Kind of indicative that I was not really seen as part of the family. I really never understand this way of thinking; fortunately, most children are not usually in the least bit interested in social class and so forth. But looking back I think I can see that the root of the problem really lay not in my being 'better' but rather, 'different'.

Many normal families produce a cuckoo, a child who is simply different in many respects from the rest of the family; but this is their cuckoo and they simply love this odd character. The cuckoo is happy being odd while the family enjoy observing this oddness. They may tease their cuckoo from time to time, as all family members are teased, but let anyone else try to tease that child and they will immediately regroup to defend it to the death.

The problem with my situation was that I was truly a cuckoo from another nest who simply just didn't match up to any of their expectations. To make matters worse, neither of my adopted parents showed any great signs of intelligence, or interest in the wider world. My father had worked hard and was very diligent but that was as far as it went. He read the newspaper while my mother flicked through magazines; they only listened to the light music of the day on the radio and a few comedy programmes, but were even quite bemused by the humour of the Goon Show. They watched such films as were shown on television but as soon as ITV became available they rarely watched the BBC again.

Strangely, Nanny had broader horizons, she read books and listened to plays and other programmes on the radio. I spent almost every evening with Nanny in those early years and we spent a lot of time searching the airwaves for interesting things to listen to. In this way we came across opera and both thought it rather splendid and wanted more of it. One evening we were both sitting with our eyes shut enraptured by a wonderful aria when the door flew open and Muriel told her mother to "Turn that dreadful caterwauling off. I can't stand it." Nanny duly obliged, which is rather odd when you think about it, since it was her house and her radio!

Looking back I think I can safely surmise that one of the major triggers was that although my mother was quite canny, as the Scots would say, she nevertheless appeared to possess a below average IQ; and I, through no fault or credit of my own, came pre-packaged with a much higher one.

Eventually it finally dawned on me that God had supplied me with a reasonable brain, despite what I had been told in the past, and I just needed to get on and learn how to use it. I have to admit that this is still a work in progress. Whilst my head may have caused me to reject the endless shouted accusations of "You're completely useless" and "You'll never amount to anything, you're so stupid" and even "You'll end up like your mother, a slut", my heart fell for it hook, line and sinker. I had to look up that last insult in the library but was still none the wiser. But when that often-made accusation finally came to mean something, the wounding was far deeper and painful than any of those physical blows that were regularly rained upon me. When you insult a child's origins you wound the most vulnerable part of their integrity, and unlike adults they have no way of defending themselves, since although the heart is screaming with pain the brain does not have the knowledge or the words to repudiate such things. It may be a cliche, but when an aggressor wants to wind up another person sufficiently enough to make them retaliate, they often resort to defaming the origins and lifestyle of that person's mother. It works a treat!

Whilst I can find no excuse for Muriel's behaviour, I can see that finding herself with a highly argumentative child who could outwit her at every point, and who would always come back for more no matter what you handed out, was the perfect recipe for disaster. I think in the end she grew to hate me, which must have made life very bitter for her. It was certainly bitter for me too, though I still managed to thoroughly enjoy myself as soon as I was away from the house. Part of the constant dread I lived with was the complete uncertainty of what to expect on a daily basis. I could walk in the door, home from school, and know the moment I stepped inside, from the very atmosphere, that no matter what I did or did not do, did or did not say, the sword of Damocles was waiting to drop. Yet other times I would be met with a smile and a drink and biscuit and be asked what I had done at school, and then ten minutes later the glass would be broken and the milk all up the wall and I would be nursing a damaged shoulder, or bruised arm, and then be shouted at to "clear up the mess you've made!" The first sign of the abatement of any temper tantrum would be the phrase "now look what you've made me do!" And inside I would be asking "well what exactly did I do?" Most of the time I could simply never work it out.

The constant uncertainty certainly took its toll. Most habits begin slowly and one day I noticed how although I always left school at a trot I stopped running after a while, and then started walking ever more slowly, by the time I reached the top of our road I was down to very tiny, very slow steps. A neighbour out in his front garden once said, "If you go much slower lass you'll be walking backwards" which is probably what I was hoping for. Home should be a place of joy, acceptance and safety, but for me it was the complete antithesis of that; and still today there are children who just don't want to go home. Keep your eyes open for them.

When I was fourteen and discovered that I could legally leave home at sixteen to join the army I decided that I would combine my desire to be a nurse with my interest in the military and join the Queen Alexandra's Royal Army Nursing Corp; strange really since I had no idea about my family's military history at that point. So I drew up a grid of about eight hundred tiny squares, one for each day left of my sentence; and duly proceeded to cross them off day by day. I never actually got to the end of that grid for reasons you will discover later, but it gave me strength to know there was a visible end to my suffering. The grid squares were tiny as it had to be kept hidden for obvious reasons, and since everything I owned was regularly opened and searched that was a difficult task. Once it was discovered, but I was able to pass it off as a game I was working on, it pays to be weird sometimes.

****

By this stage you may be wondering why I never asked for help; or why my teachers and others didn't notice the marks and bruises. There are probably several reasons for this apparent oversight. Despite the workhouses having long been closed, and orphanages having been changed into what aimed to be decent children's homes, there was still the hint of stigma for a child that had somehow managed to disengage themselves from their parents. Still the echo of Lady Bracknell saying "To lose one parent, Mr. Worthing, may be regarded as a misfortune; to lose both looks like carelessness". Over the years I did try a few times to let people know what was going on, but not only was it a waste of time but it just rebounded on me and made things worse. I might stutter out something about being frightened of being hit, kicked, and shouted at all the time, and this seemingly kind person who had just asked you why you seemed upset, rounded on you with accusations of you being an "Ungrateful, wicked child; telling lies about your nice parents who have given you a lovely home." If it ever got back to my mother that I had said such things, well of course she would stop. But only long enough to catch her breath and prepare herself for an onslaught that would teach me never to try anything like that again. Besides, as already mentioned, it was still considered imprudent to interfere in any but the most outrageous of domestic incidents, and that usually had to include a dead body.

Many years later I was to discover a far more sinister reason for my never being believed on the rare occasions I took the risk to speak out, and which was probably why Muriel got away with meeting out years of abuse. It just so happened that in the early days of social media I was contacted through Friends Reunited by an old school friend that I had lost touch with years before. Like me she had been a Girl Guide. She was still in touch with our old Guide Captain and invited me to a reunion back in Redhill; at that stage we were living in Hastings in Sussex. When I arrived I was disappointed to find that my friend was unable to attend due to illness and that all the women who were there, were from a much younger set than mine and I didn't know any of them. However, Captain was delighted to see me and asked me to meet up with her later for a meal before I drove home. This we duly did and had a great time looking back at some lovely times at camps and so on. I apologised to her for being such a pain, because despite loving school, church and guides I was always in and out of trouble. "Oh that's alright" she responded "You were never unkind or malicious; quite funny actually! Besides, I knew why you behaved like that."

At this my mouth dropped open and I remember feeling sick and then going cold all over. I had trusted and respected this woman, yet she had known what was going on in my life for years and acted as if nothing was happening; I just couldn't process this.

"Yes" she went on "Your mother explained it all to me before I even met you." If it's possible for a heart to both rise and sink at the same time, then mine did just that. She went on to explain that while I was still being fostered Muriel had come

46

to her to sign me up to join the Brownie pack at our local church, Captain was Brown Owl at the time and moved up to being Guide Captain at about the same time as I moved up to Guides. Muriel had explained that they were waiting to adopt me and that I had been put into care because my mother had ill-treated me to such an extent that the police were involved. Worse still, as soon as I arrived at Barnardo's I been sent to a foster family that also ill-treated me before returning me to the home. Well my mother may not have managed five-star child-care but I don't ever remember her hurting me, she just tended to ignore us. We were taken into care because she was ill, not cruel. Neither do I have any recollections of a bad foster home; I actually only had a few short stays in a few homes. I have no recollection of ever being mistreated until Muriel laid hands on me. But this horrible history, she told Captain, was the reason why I told stories and believed that I was still being badly treated and that people were hurting me. Also, to compound the lie, it was added that I had something wrong with me that made me bruise easily. As if that was not enough, she was told that, despite having dance lessons, I was a very clumsy and uncoordinated child and was always hurting myself. Being worried that people might misinterpret this Muriel was letting her know and hoped she would make sure the word was passed on. Now that the secret was out my gullible Guide leader said that she did indeed quite understand, and discretely let others at church and elsewhere know the situation.

By this stage of the conversation my face must have spoken volumes because tears started to slide down Captain's face. "It wasn't true was it?" she gasped. I told her a little of the truth, but not too much since it really had not been her fault, and she was clearly ashamed of being so naïve. The drive from Redhill to Hastings takes just over an hour and I remember it being a very long and painful hour. I was trying to come to terms with the realisation that my almost daily torture throughout my childhood was not just the by-product of someone who was sick and could not perhaps help themselves, but rather a premeditated plan designed to safeguard themselves from any possibility that people might work out what was really happening. This was somebody who knew they were unable to control their temper and probably were not safe to care for a small child and yet intended to do just that. I had been set up before I had barely arrived on the scene. Looking back it's easy to see that the same story was probably peddled to my teachers and any other adults I came into contact with; hence the mixed, but always negative reactions I met when I tried to ask for help.

There were days when I had to promise to keep my cardigan on all day, despite the hot weather, and other times when I had to take a note for the PE teacher to say that I wasn't too well and couldn't do PE that day. This was the ultimate disappointment for me as I loved PE and games, as far as I was concerned this was what school existed for. I did also love history, music, and English, and especially poetry, but PE, in all its forms was my main focus. Nothing could offer solace for having to watch others play the games that I loved; and often they would have been happy enough to swap with me and sit out. Actually, I did bruise quite easily, which was unfortunate for Muriel, because although she usually went for body blows, where marks wouldn't be visible, she still needed to catch me first. Not surprisingly I didn't stand still and wait to be hit, we even ended up at times running round the table as if we were performing in a slapstick silent movie; but she usually caught me in the end by grabbing an arm and gripping me hard before the final assault began, and finger marks are fairly obvious on a child's skin. She eventually went for the safer way of grabbing me by the hair, which makes you quite powerless; that was probably why I always wanted short hair.

There was one occasion when we arrived at dance class and I changed into my tunic whilst she was talking to someone. So I suddenly found myself being stared at by a lot of adults who must have been shocked at the marks on my arms - very obviously handprints. Muriel certainly managed to think fast on that occasion "oh dear, look at that, she's such a clumsy child she nearly fell downstairs yesterday and her daddy only just managed to grab her in time." Since I was usually singled out to do a solo at the dance shows twice a year, it's unlikely that my dance teacher considered me clumsy, yet she believed what she was told. I can only hope and pray that people are more alert these days, and more prepared to speak out if concerned about a child.

You may be wondering why I didn't take my jumper, off at school, as visual evidence of abuse is hard to deny. Well to understand that you have to know both the mind of a child and the mind of an abuser. As a child I had no idea that adults would feel sorry for me, I assumed that most parents behaved like that at times, after all most children got 'smacked' in those day, a slap on the leg or the bottom to bring us to our senses. I was occasionally issued one of those by a teacher and, apart from the humiliation, it never bothered me; after all, I had committed the crime and was only getting what I had been warned about, and so it was justified, and also so very different from what I received at home. No, I assumed they would be appalled to see just how naughty I must have been to deserve such punishment, and would probably never allow their children to talk to me again.

But there were some people who were more aware of the situation I lived with each day. I did endure digestive problems which plagued me throughout my childhood, problems that have never really gone away, but I also suffered from what are now known as dissociative seizures. I had these non-epileptic fits for a period of around six or seven years. Sometimes I could go for some months without any and then suffer a whole cluster of them. I would never know when they were coming and I would just have the embarrassment of waking up to find myself on the floor staring up at the faces of worried people. I clearly remember the first one. I was around eleven and had just come home from school to find my Uncle and Auntie were visiting, I don't know if they had been arguing between themselves, but I could certainly sense an atmosphere.

Muriel asked me what I had been doing at school, and as is the case with most youngsters, somewhere between school and home I had switched off the school part of my brain and could not remember a thing. Simply because I couldn't answer her question she set about teaching me my manners, it was almost as if she had completely forgotten that others were present; perhaps in her outrage she had. All this was going on in a small hallway at the foot of the stairs and I remember trying to escape up the stairs whilst Muriel yanked me backwards by my hair whilst punching me in the back. The next thing I remember was finding myself on the floor and thinking I must have been asleep, but wondering why Muriel's head was wobbling, as I came too I realised it was because Uncle Fred was shaking her hard and Auntie Hilda was screaming at her to leave me alone. I do wonder if it ever crossed their minds to wonder just what might be going on when no one else was present.

These kinds of fits are much better understood these days, and it's not difficult to imagine that my brain had discovered that one way of escaping a situation that was seemingly inescapable was simply to shut the system down, after all it might provide protection and it certainly meant you were no longer aware of what was going on. Recent research suggests once the brain gets into this kind of escape mechanism it can't always distinguish between a real threat and the perceived threat of a bad memory. This might explain why I could be having a great time out and about when I would suddenly flake out, presumably an ugly memory had been triggered in conversation that my brain decided it didn't want to cope with. I don't know quite how many times my life was actually endangered but on two occasions I lost consciousness whilst swimming, once in the sea and once in a swimming pool. Both times I was with people, and I think I came to as soon as water was rushing down my throat, but not a pleasant experience. The good thing was that my brain eventually decided to do the right thing and stop responding to stress in that way as soon as it recognised my body was carrying new life.

****

If you've ever seen the film *Fanny by Gaslight* you will know to what extraordinary lengths some people will go, to cloak and dissemble their abuse of another person, and to persuade the victim that they are so bad that they deserve everything that comes to them. The story spun to my Guide Captain was not uncovered until I was an adult, but another situation impinged on me very early on in the proceedings taught me just how dangerous the idea of letting things slip would be.

During my fourth to seventh years while I lived in Redhill, both during my foster period and even for a year or so after the adoption, I was visited every few months by people from Barnardo's, who came to see how things were going. This was before the days of email and even before we had our own phone, so a letter would be sent giving the date and time of the visit some weeks ahead of the event. How convenient Muriel must have found this. It meant for a week or two, apart from a bit of screaming and shouting, there were no hits, punches or kicks. An hour before the expected time of arrival, always during the day when Thomas was at work, I would be put into a new dress, given a new toy to play with, and sat on a chair to listen to the same set of instructions issued prior to each visit. "Only answer 'yes' or 'no', if they ask you if you are happy and want to stay here say 'yes, I'm very happy thank you' – and don't forget I will hear everything and if you say anything that I don't like, when they've gone I will kill you."

At the appointed time two nice ladies - probably related to the two nice ladies from the Fairbridge Society - would arrive, be given a cup of tea and a biscuit, and settle themselves down to ask me a few questions. Do you remember the painting *When did you last see your Father?* by William Frederick Eames?

Then you can imagine the scene. I'm sitting on one side of a table, and the two nice ladies are sitting opposite me. Muriel is standing just behind them glaring at me. Since I never believed or understood for one moment that they would do anything if I told them I was unhappy and wanted to go back to St Christopher's, I had no plans to spill the beans. I had been told I would be punished or killed if I said anything wrong so I did my utmost not to say anything out of order. Even so, the slightest hesitation earned a scowl from across the room. On more than one occasion one of them might turn a look at Muriel who would immediately flash a big smile. Even aged four or five, I instinctively knew this was not the way things were meant to be, but these two professional people seemingly sensed nothing odd about the situation. Years later, when I spoke with a representative of Barnardo's I was given an apology and assured that home visits were now usually unexpected and much more rigorous, the child would be interviewed separately for example. For that, I'm truly grateful. After each of these visits things quickly returned to normal the next day and it was business as usual.

When I was just coming up for my eighth birthday I was told I was going to be adopted, I didn't really understand what that meant, but there was a tendency for adults not to explain much to children in those days, and my parents were the sort to not even try; so it was all a bit of mystery. The allocated day came round and I was surprised to be told that my father had a day off work and I had a day off school. The fact that I was dressed up in new outfit probably roused my suspicions but it turned out we were going on a nice bus ride to Reigate.

When we got there we went into one of those big 'official' buildings that I was by now moderately familiar with. After a lot of hanging around, we ended up in a huge room with lots of people milling about and carrying things backwards and forwards. I was rather amazed as I looked around to see an old man wearing a red dressing gown sitting in a wooden box that was fixed halfway up the wall – did he need a ladder to reach it? Even more surprising was that he apparently hadn't noticed that he had a piece of sheepskin on top of his head! People wearing black dressing gowns were talking in a strange language to each other and occasionally to my parents.

Suddenly I nearly jumped out of my skin when the man in the box on the wall boomed down at me "So Dorothy, these nice people want to be your new mummy and daddy, isn't that lovely?" I think he was expecting an answer, but shock and fear rendered me speechless. I desperately wanted to say 'No' and risk the inevitable outcome but I just could not make my mouth work. So my no response was taken as an affirmative; would they have done anything had I managed to say 'No' anyway? I somehow doubt it.

Standing at the bus stop waiting for the bus back to Redhill I started to sob, and despite being told off because I was supposed to be happy, I continued to sob all the way home. Although only a young child I had a strong sense of self, and it had dawned on me that, completely without my request or consent I had just lost the only things that were truly mine, my name and my identity. I sobbed in secret for weeks to come.

I reiterate what Jinling Wu said in March 2021:

Adoption is not simple . . . adoptees that spoke out with anything other than gratitude were ostracised by a society that only sees the value of adoption without recognising the trauma.

Here is someone who knows where I was coming from!

Escape to School

Barnardo's, having a Christian foundation, and in keeping with most institutions of the time, taught us Bible stories and songs; and when I arrived in Redhill I was signed up to a church school and Sunday school simply because my mother had bequeathed this when she signed me over for adoption – I very much doubt if it would have happened that way without Barnardo's insistence. So I have them to thank for my wonderfully ecumenical training. My first school was St Matthew's Redhill, a Church of England infants and primary school attached to one of the town parishes, which happened to be quite high Anglo-Catholic in practice, whereas the church where I went to Sunday School was of the Anglican Evangelical persuasion. All of which meant nothing to me of course, I just enjoyed the seasonal colours and music of St Matthew's and the training and pastoral care at Holy Trinity.

I don't quite remember how I came to be a member of the church choir; I know I was one of the youngest for some time and that most of the other dozen or so children weren't actually from St Matthews school. I have so many lovely memories of my four or five years as a chorister.

One of my most 'sensory' memories of this time is coming home after the midnight service one Christmas Eve, well Christmas Morning by then. I walked through the town just as a frost was beginning to sparkle on the pavements, some festive lights were still on, and now and then the merry sound of some distant late-night revellers floated on the air. It was so cold that the ground was hard and the sound of my footsteps rang as I walked. Singing carols to myself I marched along, seeing my breath in the air as I gazed up looking for the star the wisemen had followed. I think I saw it. I've always loved Christmas and all the fond memories that it brings with it, but I doubt if I'll ever experience such magic again on this earth.

We were well trained as a choir having a practice session one night each week and learned how to read music along with pronunciation and correct breathing and so forth. I really believe it's something that all children should be encouraged to experience – it's a great foundation for so many of the performing arts. Strangely perhaps, I also loved the solemnity and the discipline. As soon as I was garbed in the appropriate attire my demeanour changed, as we stood waiting in line in the vestry ready to process into the service I was ready to play the part. I probably wouldn't have understood the term professional, but I knew how to be it. Like most of my family, acting was in my genes and I was always mystified by many of my peers who didn't seem to understand appropriate behaviour. I remember being horrified by other children who, in school productions or concerts, would be actively looking around for their family and then actually wave at them! I did not need to be told to keep playing the role until well off stage – that was obvious wasn't it?

Those talents meant that I was a favourite with some teachers, but with others, I was undoubtedly deemed as hopeless, or worse. Putting aside having mild dyslexia and ADHD (which weren't recognised in those days and so didn't actually exist of course) I did find it so hard to concentrate on the mundane, and particularly when we were often required to learn from just the printed word without any visual stimulus at all. How I envy the visual way in which children are taught today - I'm always learning new skills by watching YouTube! Once I had heard the words or understood the concept I could usually remember it well, but for some years it was just so hard to get it into my head in the first place. Most of the time what I wanted was a very earnest one to one conversation on the subject with the teacher and the means to go off at relevant tangents when required. Strangely enough, that wasn't what most teachers required of me and I was quite unable to produce the goods in the prescribed way as required by the system.

I have always loved poetry and had a good memory for songs and poems. Probably a great deal to do with the choir training. As usual, I had to go a step further than required and always learned the words of any choral piece by heart so that I could follow the conductor and not look down at the words. Over the years I have committed a large number of songs and hymns to memory, and I find it very comforting to be able to call them to mind when I'm in pain or just can't sleep.

I certainly went beyond the call of duty in school when our English teacher, who was a Sunday School teacher at my 'other 'church, and with whom I got on very well, asked us to learn a poem from the class poetry reader for the next week in order to recite them to each other. This was made up of either short poems and ditties or a few verses from some of the more epic poems. No sooner had I received the instructions than I was rifling through the book with great excitement. What caught my eye was some verses about badly behaved rats. This clearly needed further investigation, so I stopped off at the Public Library on my way home, which was a detour I made two or three times a week, to have a chat with my favourite librarian. She immediately found the full version of *The Pied Piper of Hamelin* by Robert Browning, clearly designed for children to enjoy since it had wonderful illustrations on every page.

By the following week I had learned all three hundred and three lines by heart. At the start of the class Miss Ladyman asked if anyone had a poem they would like to present. I gave that recital my all, including character voices and actions, and got a hearty round of applause at the end. Since I must have taken up nearly half the lesson most of it was probably relief from my peers that I had lessened their chances of being called upon. But nobody seemed to notice one very strange thing, and that was throughout the whole performance I didn't stutter once; given that I had an intermittent but quite severe stutter throughout most of my childhood you would have thought that someone might have spotted that. Some teachers were very supportive and patient, some were not. Despite my love of literature one teacher nearly wrecked it for me.

Fast forward to my secondary school. It was another English Literature class, but this was quite different. This teacher followed the practice of reading round the class whatever book we were set to study. At the beginning of each lesson one hapless student was called upon to stand up and start reading at the required page and read until the command "change" was issued. At this she would be allowed to sit down while the girl either next to her or behind her, would stand up and continue reading. Depending on the size of the class there were usually some fortunate people who managed to avoid getting the chance to read to us. If possible I always sat in the back row, as far away from authority as possible.

For someone who was always very short-sighted, it's somewhat surprising that I didn't get my first pair of glasses until I was fourteen; I was never able to read what was on the board and so always had to either copy from my neighbour or make it up as I went along, even when sitting near the front of the classroom, and I was always being told off at home for sitting too near the television and blocking other people's view. Eventually the school sent me for an eye test, having assured my parents that they wouldn't have to pay for glasses. I vividly remember the day I went to collect them. They were duly tried on in the shop, declared fit for purpose, and I set off home wearing them - except I nearly didn't get home. As I was crossing the road I made the mistake of looking up, and there I found myself actually seeing clouds for the first time. Oh the detail, the artwork! Forgetting everything, including that I was standing in the middle of the A23 London to Brighton trunk road, I stood gazing at the wonder of such beauty whilst cars and lorries swerved around me.

One of the main reasons for always heading for the desk at the back right corner of the room was that the first reader picked was usually at the front left of the room, right in front of the teacher's desk - all very predictable. I had soon worked out that if we ran out of time I was likely not to have been called to read. This also meant that, being the annoying child that I was, I could hide my book in my lap and read ahead, I had usually finished the book whilst the rest of the class was still on the third chapter. This was risky but if it were an interesting book I could usually remember enough to respond well to any trick question on what had just been read, but even this skill could not save me from the 'terror'. Again, I was aware of the inexorable, the passing of the baton around the classroom to my desk, and as my turn to read drew closer I started to feel sick and would then find myself shaking and breaking out in a sweat. What was confronting me was nothing like as harsh and violent as I experienced on a regular basis at home, but that usually came upon me suddenly and the responding adrenaline rush helped me cope with it, this was simply the overwhelming knowledge that something inescapable was bearing down on you.

Had I been asked to read without any prior warning I probably would have managed quite well. If I had been able to see it as a performance opportunity, as I had done with the poem, I might have felt equal to the task, but the problem was that we were expected to read exactly what was in front of us. Now anyone who has ever had a stutter will know that it has absolutely nothing to do with the tongue not being able to speak the actual words, it is some kind of misfiring in the brain that deceives you into thinking that there are certain words, or letters, that you just cannot say at this particular time. Although you may well be able to manage saying these self-same words at other times. The more you struggle the harder the whole thing becomes.

My particular *bêtes noir* was anything that began with the letter 'A', which just happens to appear quite often at the beginning of sentences and paragraphs. If I had been free to start reading in a different place, or even add a few ad-libs such as "Now dear reader" or even "Well . . ." as you might in performance mode, it would have made life a lot easier. But a hawk-eyed, and fussy teacher does not allow for such prevarications. One in particular, seemed to be quite convinced that I was just a complete pest, and that this was just another way I had of showing off. No matter how quickly I launched off halfway through the first sentence, or how small the changes I made to the text I would be hauled back to start over again. There I would stand with either nothing coming out of my mouth, or strange gargling sounds. Even employing the trick that seemed to work of a quick cough added to the first word would infuriate her. I am sure that she was quite convinced I was just being silly or trying to annoy, but had she taken the time to listen to me speaking in other contexts she might have picked up on that stutter. Certainly it was worse some days than others but it was there right into my twenties, and still makes an occasional appearance, which of course surprises people who have heard me addressing an audience, class or congregation with barely a flicker.

Something which should not have been a surprise, but which took my own children to point out to me was the correlation between my adopted mother and my stutter. As an adult with my own family, on the odd occasion Muriel would ring me I would immediately revert to being tongue-tied and struggling to overcome it. When Carolyn was around fourteen she said in passing "oh we can always tell when you answer the phone to 'Eastbourne' "as they called her "because your stutter starts immediately". A few years after that I 'divorced' my mother (more on that later) and I have to say that now it's only when I'm badly stressed or very tired, that my stutter ever bothers to put in a half-hearted appearance.

Despite these frustrations I so loved drama and music, and for that my secondary school of choice, Bishop Simpson C of E Girls School in Redhill, was ideal. It was still in the process of being built when I started there and was one of the new 'secondary moderns' that were just being introduced. Such schools were essentially designed to give an all-round secondary level education fit for the large numbers of manual and office workers required for the labour market. To be fair, even in an all-girls school where learning to type and domestic science skills were seen as important, we still had a good choice of subjects. Many chose to learn languages and sciences and some students did go on to further and even higher education. Being a flagship school in which the Church of England had made a huge investment, it was well equipped with all modern facilities and especially in the theatre, music and sports departments. In fact, we were so well supplied and had such a good reputation of being a 'nice' school, that a number of girls who had successfully passed the eleven plus had opted to attend rather than go to grammar school. Many travelled some distance, so great was the school's appeal. It is quite likely that there were still many parents in those days who thought it more fitting for girls to have a more domestic education in a nice school than to undertake a more rigorous academic education. I suppose it was more the equivalent of a modern-day academy. Ironically, I ended up serving as a governor on the board of a Church of England Academy in later life.

We had a wide range of musical instruments at our disposal and we were encouraged to take them home to practice. I think a few of the teaching staff were well connected since barely a month went by without a visitation from a famous actor, scientist, sports person or musician. Indeed Benjamin Britten put in regular appearances and used quite a few of us as cast for a huge television production of his *Noye's Fludde* in Reigate Priory. I learned to play all of the recorder family and spent many hours a week practising and learning new pieces from sheet music supplied by school.

We sometimes played cricket in the summer, which was probably unusual for girls back then, but my favourite sport was rounders. Perhaps it was all the tennis lessons I had had over the years, but I had a good eye and could really annoy visiting teams by whacking that ball out of the park. I ended up representing the county in both rounders and hurdling. I was no sprinter or distance runner but hurdles worked for me, for a while at least. When I started to train I was probably only a tad shorter than most other girls my age, and so could manage the both the height of the hurdles and the three steps in between them. After a few years, however, the others had grown a few inches and so could cope with the increase in the height and distance between the hurdles that made things age appropriate. I hadn't grown, and so I either had to do five tiny steps, or four very long ones which meant alternating the leading leg. So my hurdling career was over I went back to concentrating on tennis.

****

When I was in the fifth grade I chose to do typing classes, most of which were held after school. We were taught very thoroughly, with the keys covered over so that we never got into the habit of looking down at the keyboard but rather up at the blackboard where both the key layout and the text we had to type were displayed. We even typed to music sometimes as it helped us gain a smooth rhythm. I am grateful for that experience to this day. All my working life I've been able to type without thinking about it, and with my eyes firmly fixed on the subject in hand. It amazes me that proper keyboarding is rarely taught these days, especially since we have made everyone so reliant on computers. The 'hunt and peck' approach that most people use, is tiring, inefficient and prone to making typos. It's a bit like giving everyone a musical instrument but never teaching them to play it!

Around that time we had a group of students from a university research group come to try out their 'auto-tutors' on us. This was mid 1960s and desktop computers wouldn't make an appearance for a few more years, so they were ahead of their times. The device was like nothing we had seen before, it was fairly large screen on the front of a box with something like a keyboard that just had A, B and C buttons and a forward button. In fact it looked just like a microfiche reader which you might still find in some libraries, but of course we had no idea of that. Given that these had been around since the early 50s this was clearly a modified version of this technology.

A lesson tape was loaded into the back of the machine and the power switched on. The screen displayed the first part of the lesson which you read and then pressed the forward button. The next screen asked you a question and presented three answers for you to choose from. When you pressed your selected button the screen automatically moved onto the next screen which either congratulated you on selecting the correct answer or told you that you had given the wrong answer, sometimes being annoyed enough to tell you that you clearly hadn't been concentrating properly! If you had the correct answer you could move forward to the next part of the lesson, if you had it wrong you were moved to a new page which gave you further and more detailed information on the subject. At the end of the lesson you were shown your score of 'correct first time' answers which were duly noted by the researchers.

One break time, when the class teacher and research student were out of the room, I set about taking the back off the machine to see how it worked. When I was about four I got my first real beating from Muriel Peters, my then temporary foster mother, for taking apart a tin windup penguin. I loved that little penguin and was very sad when I couldn't put it together again, but I had started to understand just a little about the stored energy of a wound-up spring! A salutary lesson, but it didn't stop me from taking apart anything of interest if I thought no one was looking!

What I found in the auto-tutor was a counter device that was tripped every time an incorrect answer was selected but not on correct answers. This, of course, was what was displayed on the screen as your final score. Being just a simple mechanism it was possible to wind it back to get a better score. When I showed it to the others we all wound our scores back, though we did have the sense to not overdo it and make it look suspicious. We did this little trick every session from then on. Having run similar research projects myself, I do find myself wondering if the results from most research is actually 100% accurate, given how many 'hidden' variables might have been included.

In all I thoroughly enjoyed my school days, despite being so often in trouble, I only wish I had been able to take from it the learning that I so longed for.

The Strangeness of Home

Even though I was regarded by many as a naughty child throughout my life I have always had an awareness of the numinous. God is there, no question of 'if' or even 'why'; God exists and is in control. This might be down to my awareness of the spiritual from my experience in the church choir, we were certainly taught about the sacredness of Christian worship. But like most children I was influenced by the fashions and fads of others. I suppose I was around ten years old when, having been told by other children that their parents had explained that the Bible was all made-up stories, and because science had proved it all wrong anyway they did not believe that God existed. I decided the time had come to join them. So I went out in the dark one night in the garden of our tiny, terraced house to tell God that I no longer believed. It was rather ironic that it was necessary for me to inform God that he was not there, but I was an honest child and felt it was the right thing to do. Standing there in the darkness I looked up at the sky and chose a bright star, this was my new divinity. I spoke a prayer to this ball of gas and went back indoors feeling very smug. How God must have chuckled, especially when I went out the next night to pray to my star, only to discover that the pesky thing had moved and I did not have a clue which star I had dedicated myself too either. Even as I went through that charade I felt like a toddler showing off - pretending their beloved parent wasn't actually watching, whilst all along knowing they were.

It would be unfair to say that as a child I wasn't provided with all that was required for a decent life – in the material sense that is, but I was certainly kept very short compared to many of my friends, and never really allowed any ownership of what were supposed to be my own possessions. Toys would appear from out of the blue, for no apparent reason, and then disappear just as suddenly. I remember a very smart baby doll appearing in the post from some cousins in America, of whom I had hitherto been quite unaware. I never really liked dolls, much-preferring teddy bears and other cuddly toys, but even I could see that this was no ordinary doll, it even had rooted hair and changes of outfit, all long before *Barbie*. I played with it a few times when there was not much else to do and then, a couple of weeks after it had arrived it disappeared. When I asked where it had gone I was told it had been given away to someone who would appreciate it. A few days later I heard Muriel telling someone what a bargain she had struck selling an American doll.

That particular episode did not particularly bother me, but one that did irk me, and still niggles me if I'm honest was my *Popeye*. Again it arrived out of the blue from America and I had to write a thank you letter to people I didn't know. I was pretty sure it was not new but it did arrive in its box. At the time it was just a toy, but I knew it was fragile, made of a sort of light-weight *Bakelite* plastic. It was a windup toy with a key in its back, which I had to be careful not to overwind. When wound it just vibrated on its flat feet which made it shuffle along the table whilst swinging its over-muscled arms and turning its head, complete with pipe in mouth, from side to side. Not terribly exciting but I was quite fond of it and managed to keep it for some years.

When I left home to get married I took very little with me, since I had very little, but left a few toys and knickknacks to be collected later - Little Ted, of course, travelled with me. When, a few months later we went down to Eastbourne to visit my parents, I asked to take the box of items I'd left in their keeping back home with me. I was informed that since it was mostly rubbish everything had either been thrown away or given away. I knew by then that the Popeye was a vintage model and quite collectable, even in those days. I also knew that Muriel often visited a local shop that bought and sold vintage toys.

It seems strange now that I learned to look after my own property, and thereby respect that of others, in a children's home. The Barnardo's nurses were very assiduous in encouraging us to take care of what was considered ours, the few personal things we had were kept in a cupboard by our bed, and yet to be generous in sharing all the rest that were considered family toys. Thus it was always a surprise to me that later my property was never really considered to be my own, letters would always be opened and read and books and toys could just disappear without a word.

When I was about eight I came out of school one day with a huge 'golly' (as they were known then) displayed in a cellophane wrapper. The school secretary had stopped me on the way out and said that my mother had won this in the school Christmas raffle, but had not been there to collect it. She saw my obvious delight in the gorgeous toy and said "You're going to enjoy playing with him aren't you?"

"Yes" I said.

"No!" said my mother when I handed it over outside the school gate "It's not yours, I paid for the ticket so it's mine". I still had to carry it all the way home. While she was cooking supper I carefully took it out of the wrapper and cut one of the buttons off its very smart jacket, having posted the button between two floorboards, I very carefully replaced the toy in its casing. When Muriel picked it up later to put it away she noticed the flaw and became really enraged that it was less than perfect; "Well you might as well have it then" she said as she threw it at me. Some things are just worth the risk!

I vividly recall the time when I was telling the truth about something that might, at first glance, have seemed quite unlikely. Muriel, believing that I was in fact lying, and was so outraged that she grabbed me by my hair and forced me into the kitchen and over to the stove where a saucepan was on the cooker heating the dog's dinner. Yes the dog had to have a cooked meal, often better than the one I was getting. She then tightly grabbed my right wrist, realised her mistake since I write with my right hand, and swapped it for my left. Holding my hand in the air she threatened that if I didn't tell her the truth she would hold my fingers in the gas flame until I did. As she pushed my fingertips, that were sticking straight out from her vice-like grip closer to the flames I very quickly considered making something up - anything just to save the day, but equally loud in my terrified brain was the voice of reason that said, I'm telling the truth, this shouldn't be happening; so I said nothing. True to her word she pushed my fingers into the flames. By now I was screaming so loudly the whole neighbourhood could have heard me, and since she was unable to stop the noise and keep up the torture at the same time, after what was probably only a couple of seconds, she let go and I escaped.

When my father came home he was deeply distressed at the state of my blistered fingers and set to bathing them in *Dettol* (ouch) coating them with *Elastoplast* ointment and dressing them with bandages. Muriel had already told him that I had been helping her cook and had scalded my fingers because of my usual clumsiness. Even so, he quietly asked me how it had happened. I told him exactly what I had been told to tell him, since I knew she would probably be listening, but the way I said it through gritted teeth, one-word-at-a-time, doubtless told him what he suspected. Though of course he never said anything - I'm sure he was more frightened of her than I was.

This took place on a Friday evening and on Monday I went to school with a bandaged hand and with Muriel accompanying me to explain to the school secretary why I wouldn't be able to do P.E. for a while. For all the reasons given above I had no intention of explaining the real cause of my injuries, but when a friend asked me in the playground what was wrong I did get rather carried away with a creative tale about how I had been playing my recorder for days on end and it had caused blisters on my fingertips. I had not realised that one of the playground supervisors was listening, she took me aside, carefully opened the dressings to take a look, she then narrowed her eyes and disappeared into the staff room. But as usual, nothing was said or done - that I was aware of at least.

The problem with the lying habit was that despite being quite good at it - my thespian nature enjoyed the creative side of it; I always knew it was wrong and I always suffered horrible pangs of guilt. Even before I came to faith I always felt terrible when I lied to anyone, except Muriel. Although it took me a while to break the habit, every lie felt like I was stabbing myself. At some stage I realised that my new instinct was to immediately tell the truth, rather than lie; even when it cost me, which it often did in the home context. But the strange thing is that this childhood habit left me with a legacy of guilt, by that I mean that I still think that people are quite unlikely to believe what I am telling them. I've prayed for healing and had others pray for me, but it's never quite left. Perhaps, just as Paul had his own particular thorn in the flesh, this is mine. I do know that I have been healed and restored in so many ways, but none of us can be made completely whole in this life.

I suppose it isn't too surprising that my reactions in that area are so muddled, I was instructed to lie and then later punished for it. When Muriel was trying to get the truth out of me - which I admit must have been hard at times - I was told over and over "if you just tell me the truth I promise not to hurt you" and over and over I believed her only to find myself flying across the room a few minutes later. The irony of it was that just a few hours earlier she could have been rehearsing with me a lie I was to tell my father to suit her purposes. I suspect the old adage of their being honour amongst thieves is complete rubbish!

****

When I was about fourteen I got a Saturday and holiday job working in Woolworths, which I thoroughly enjoyed. It was some time before I discovered that my peers saw what they earned as their own, and did what they pleased with it. I remember a friend telling me that she enjoyed sometimes buying little things for her Mum and Gran, especially after a holiday stint, and then asked me if I ever did that. I recall the incredulous look on her face when I told her that that would be difficult since I had to give every penny I earned directly to my mother the minute I got home, I also had to produce the wage slip to prove that I hadn't 'pinched' anything! I did occasionally get something back but very little and very rarely.

Once in a moment of madness, I threw all caution to the wind and splashed out and spent half a day's wage before going home. I often walked through the town during my lunchbreak and saw that a Chinese Restaurant had just opened, very new and exciting for Redhill, and was offering a cheap three-course worker's lunch. Too good to refuse, in I went and had the time of my life. I had never been treated with such respect and was made to feel like royalty. The delight of that experience set me up for a lifelong enjoyment of Chinese cuisine. Sadly, the experience of explaining what I had done when I got home was not at all delightful. I was met with a mixture of outrage that I had spent her money on something so silly, astonishment that it should enter my head to do such a thing, and further outrage that I dared to see myself as the kind of person who eats out alone, and on a Saturday! Not once was I asked if I had enjoyed it, or what did I think of Chinese food. It was many days before she would even deem to speak to me again - which was fine by me.

In case you're wondering if Muriel needed the money more than I did, I have to put it in the context of someone who took two holidays a year, bought herself at least one new dress a month, and spent a small fortune on a constant supply of chocolates and other luxuries which were never shared with anyone else. I once was hit around the head with a very large bar of Cadbury Dairy Milk because I had dared to pinch one square from another mammoth bar that had already been opened. She set too with such vigour that it wasn't long before both wrapper and foil started coming off the bar. I suppose such an experience should have put me off chocolate for life, but it didn't!

It took me a long time to get used to generosity. The first few times I visited Michael in his parent's home in Islington I always asked if I could have a glass of water, and felt outrageous asking if I could possibly have a small glass of milk. I remember Michael's mother looking at me with amazement and saying "If it's the fridge or cupboard you can have it; once it's all gone, you can't!" Years later when we would hear our front door open and the patter of feet heading towards the kitchen, whilst we tried to work out which one of our friends was calling out "It's me, I'm just putting the kettle on," I would relish again the delight that open-handedness brings into your life.

Growing in Faith

In a sermon entitled *The Imperfections of Human Knowledge* John Wesley implied that he believed that children do not have an innate knowledge of God. He argued that our understanding of God is limited to 'what He has written in all his works, not from what He has written in our hearts' and therefore suggests that the notion that God has 'stamped . . . an idea of himself on every human soul' is unfounded. Actually, I couldn't disagree more profoundly; but then one can only ever speak in terms of one's own experience. Any knowledge we receive from others through writing or general discourse is always second-hand. But I do know that my heart was fully cognisant of God long before I had the means to express it or even understand it.

For reasons that I have never understood I grew up always aware of God being there and knowing that He cared about me. Considering how difficult my childhood was I'm doubly grateful for that privilege, which I gradually began to realise was not the default setting for all people. For many years it was my understanding that everyone knew there was a God – what they chose to do with Him was, of course, up to them; but by my middle teens I realised that this was not necessarily so, there were some people who really had no notion about God and weren't particularly bothered about it. Recently our daughter was telling about taking a six-year-old out for a walk. Having just submitted a PhD thesis entitled *Children and Holiness* she should have been prepared, but even she was amazed when the little girl asked "so before God did the creation and the universe and everything, what colour was it?"

Between them they decided that it was sort of rainbow white, since white contains all colours.

That was just the sort of thing that bothered my six-year-old head. But natural curiosity is not a relationship, and that is exactly what I have had all of my life. I have grown up knowing that I have a heavenly Father. I'm sure my Barnardo's experience must have influenced me along with school, church and choir etc., but I've met numbers of folk who grew up in very similar contexts but who never felt close to Him and thus let go of whatever relationship they might have had quite easily as the adult world impinged on them. However that was not my experience, on the contrary, I have no idea why I have been so blessed but there has never been a day in my life when I haven't believed in God – haven't known His presence. Don't misunderstand me, there have been many days and long periods when I have wanted *not* to believe in God, but I somehow never achieved it – it would be easier to doubt my own existence.

Since every one of us is totally unique then I guess that our spiritual journeys are all quite unique. I can only tell you my story and bear witness to the fact that God has always been there for me, and that I have always been aware of it. But being aware of the speed limit on the motorway doesn't always make you a dutiful driver! Yes, I have attended the naughty driver's school both literally and spiritually! As I've mentioned, going to Church services and events was like a desert dweller regularly visiting an oasis. I felt safe, happy, stimulated and respected.

Our vicar, for most of my time at Holy Trinity Redhill, was the Revd Cyril Bridgeland and it was only years later that I realised what a big part he played in my spiritual and even general education. If you attended Holy Trinity Church, as soon as you started secondary school you were invited to join Caleb Club. This took place nearly every school holiday including half-terms and usually lasted two to three days. These were designed to give the youngsters who attended a good grounding in theology, help us develop our music, worship and leadership skills, alongside having some fun. The day lasted from 9am to 3pm and was a mix of Bible study and teaching, learning new songs and writing our own, interspersed with a great lunch and a game of football, cricket or rounders. For the last twenty minutes or so Cyril would round up the day's teaching with a short discussion session and then send us on our way - unless you were one of his 'serious students' who had been quietly invited to stay on when the others left. The lovely ladies who had provided our slap-up lunch now provided tea and cake and tidied up, whilst Cyril spent anything from an hour to two hours with three or four of us in an in-depth discussion. Nothing was out of bounds and you never felt silly voicing your opinions. Oh that all young people could be so privileged and so encouraged; I was able to learn in my teens what many adults have never had the time or opportunity to explore.

Over a period of six years I must have attended around twenty such sessions, much to the great annoyance of Muriel, who hated my strong connections with my church family. Though to be fair, it was asking a lot of holiday time to be sacrificed, and since I was counted as a 'serious student' from the offset, I was out for the whole day. You might be wondering why she allowed me to go to Caleb Club for years on end, well I think I eventually worked it out. Every youngster who was a member of the church fellowship or attended the church youth group was sent an invitation in the post. When mine arrived it was duly opened in my absence and put in the waste bin; when I asked if I could attend - well let's just say the answer was negative. The next time I saw Mr Bridgeland he asked if I would be coming to his new venture. "I'd like to" I informed him "but I'm not allowed". He lowered his eyebrows and then quietly said "tell your mother that I shall be visiting her at 10.00 on Tuesday morning".

The Revd Cyril was only about five foot four and quite slight, but what he lacked in stature he made up for with a powerful presence. Nobody ever argued with Mr Bridgeland and he duly turned up on Tuesday morning. I don't know what passed between them as I was sent to do the shopping but when I came home he had left and I was told "of course you can go to this training thing - whoever said you couldn't?" I do know that Muriel made the mistake of mentioning the Barnardo's church attendance clause to him at some stage shortly after he arrived in Redhill and was visiting all the parents of Sunday School members; I know this because I was present at the time and it was the first time that I learned of my mother's church attendance legacy. It would seem quite likely that Cyril had remembered this and had no compunction about using it as a means of persuasion. However he managed it, I'm grateful to this day that he did. Spending two or three days with other youngsters studying and playing together, in the presence of lovely people who fed me and showed me kindness, and even respect, was overwhelmingly wonderful to my hungry little heart.

If Caleb Club seemed like I was camping in the Elysian fields, then Holiday Club seemed like very heaven itself. The Bridgeland family had moved to Redhill a year or so after I had arrived. I've no doubt that Mr Bridgeland had attended his fair share of camps and beach missions, as Evangelical Christians did in those days. It was pretty much seen as a duty, but in truth was known to be enormous fun. Many young people who served as team members on Children's Special Service Mission camps and holiday clubs were quite convinced that the initials actually stood for Come Single Soon Married. And so one of Mr Bridgeland's first projects was to set up a week-long summer Holiday Club. Children of all ages turned up morning and afternoon for fun and games, teaching and singing. On Saturday there were barbeques and events to which parents were invited and the week culminated in a huge Family Service on Sunday morning. All of this was done in the open-air, weather permitting.

I attended every Holiday Club from the first, right through from age six to age eleven when I was allowed to become a 'junior helper'; and by the time I was fifteen I had reached the exalted rank of 'junior leader'. As part of the leadership team we met before the children arrived for a time of prayer and the team briefing, Then we had a cup of coffee before the fun and games began on the church lawn. Some years the platform would be an ark, or a train, whatever was fitting for the theme of the week. There was a talk and lots of singing and wonderfully funny skits performed by the young leaders. When that part was over we broke up into teams for the various age groups, from infants through to mid-teens; each group of around twenty or so would have an adult leader or two and some junior leaders. Dozens of members of the congregation would turn up in their cars to ferry some of these groups to such places as Reigate Hill, or a local swimming pool, whilst other groups stayed in the church grounds or walked up the road to the school games fields for a variety of boisterous games.

Muriel once, quite justifiably, complained that "you only come home to sleep during Holiday Club week". Too right, if I could have taken my sleeping bag and slept in the church porch I would have done.

Mr Bridgeland died in the 90's but the legacy he began in 1956 endures to this day and the summer Holiday Club still features large in the life of Holy Trinity Redhill. When I look back over those years those summer weeks glow like a string of precious gems on an otherwise dark background. It wouldn't be fanciful to say that no sooner had Holiday Club ended than I started counting the days to the next one, it kept me going through the year. And at that stage I had no idea just what treasures were to come my way in this context.

One of the leaders of Holiday Club was Arthur Banks, I think he or his wife had known my father some years before in a working context. They lived nearby and were perhaps the nearest my parents ever got to having friends. So fast-forward to the summer of 1970 when Michael and I returned to Holiday club with one-year-old baby Carolyn. Arthur was leading the morning event and I remember not concentrating too much since I was watching Carolyn who was already toddling around and getting into mischief. But when I heard him say "I'm going to sing you a song written by a great new

Christian singer and songwriter called Len Magee" well, then my ears pricked up! When I thanked him afterwards for playing my brother's music, he was dumbfounded. He knew I was adopted but as far as he knew I didn't know my family, and anyway this young man he was talking about was a converted drug addict who had grown up in Australia. How could I possibly think I was related to him? It took some time to explain to Arthur just some of the amazing things that had brought this to pass.

I was never afraid of telling God that I wasn't happy with the situation, and usually felt that he understood and was moving me towards a better life. I remember one Sunday afternoon I lay on my bed sobbing and saying to Him "and no one even cares that I'm hurting so much!" I felt Him say "I do, and I keep all your tears in a bottle". That took me by surprise and I remember thinking "well it must be a big bottle"! Years later I was amazed when I came across these words in Psalm 56:

You keep track of all my sorrows
You have collected all my tears in your bottle
You have recorded each one in your book

****

When I was sixteen I went on a Girl Covenantor holiday with my friends from Holy Trinity. We spent two weeks in a rather spartan boy's boarding school in Colwyn Bay in Wales, with a crowd of girls from other parts of the country. Since I was away from home I had the time of my life, despite falling out of a barn loft on my second day and badly spraining my ankle. At the end of the holiday we walked to the top of Snowdon on a bright sunny day, though it was more of a limp in my case. Since I felt so much more comfortable in my tennis shoes I 'forgot' to change into my sensible boots before getting on the coach and my error was only spotted by one of the leaders as we were halfway up the mountain. By the time we reached the top the weather had completely changed and a cold wet mist descended on us. To make matters worse I and two friends got separated from the main party and we had to make our way down on our own. By the time we were found wandering on the lower slopes by a search party we were on the verge of hypothermia, not helped in my case by soaking wet feet. It seems that we had taken hours longer than everyone else to descend since we had spiralled our way down the mountain. I never fully understood those looks of relief on the faces of our leaders when we finally returned to the coach, or the extreme annoyance we were greeted with, until years later I found myself playing the part of the adult in a similar scenario.

During that holiday a friend and I had become friendly with two boys, about our age, who lived on the school estate. They had been quite delighted to find that a large party of girls was visiting them that summer. I got on really well with one of the boys in particular and when he asked if we could continue our friendship by writing to each other, I vaguely said that I would knowing full well that I probably wouldn't since every incoming letter was opened. As our coach left the school drive for the home journey and we waved goodbye to the boys I felt very sad, partly to be leaving such a happy environment and partly because I knew what I was going back to. My brief friendship with Rob had shown me what might be possible, at least for other people. I felt so lonely and remember leaning my head against the coach window and praying "Lord, please send me someone to love".

When I told Michael about that prayer, years later, he was amazed that - given the circumstances I was living in - that I hadn't prayed "Lord, please send someone to love me". But God gives wisdom to his children when they are genuinely crying out to him, and I instinctively knew that being able to truly love someone would be my healing.

That holiday took place just a week or so before Holiday Club. By this stage the event had grown to quite a size with a team of around thirty to forty helpers, most of whom lived locally. The previous year, when I had been fifteen, I had found it quite amusing to watch the girls around my age and a little older getting excited about two young men from London who joined us. Before Mr Bridgeland moved to Redhill he had been the vicar of Holy Trinity Islington. Knowing that a couple of lads from his old church were on their holidays from University he had summoned the two 'Michael's' to attend. Michael Wells was teacher training at Goldsmiths College, University of London, and Michael Eaton was training for the ministry and coming to Redhill as the new curate. I think it was that year that he met one of the teacher's at my school, Jenny Woods, and they ended up marrying and living and ministering in Nairobi, Kenya. Michael went on to write many theological tomes.

I have two abiding memories of Miss Woods. Since we went to the same church she would often spend time talking with me, which of course meant that I liked her straight away. She was my 'domestic science' teacher, as it was termed then, and basically taught me how to cook and plan meals. One afternoon about six of us were sitting around her desk taking notes from the board as she wrote. On the table in front of us were a hundred or more beautifully made petit four biscuits, spread out on cooling racks; which, Miss Woods informed us were for the School Governor's meeting that would convene after classes had ended.

As I looked up to see what Miss Woods was writing I happened to spot the girl at the other end of the row snaffle a biscuit and pop it in her mouth. A minute or so later the next girl did the same and so on until it was obviously my turn. Well, I wasn't going to be chicken and besides they did look quite irresistible, so the next time Miss Woods was writing I popped one into my mouth. Even as I did so she immediately turned around and looked straight at me, "*you* should know better" was all she said before turning back to continue her work. Suddenly that one innocent little biscuit increased to the size of a small monolith and practically choked me. To the mystification of the other girls, I sat with tears streaming down my bright red face. Lesson well taught.

****

It was a couple of months after Holiday Club 1961 when I was sitting in the church hall at a meeting for all those intending to participate in some way in next year's event, that I noticed something. What I saw as I sat there observing people speaking, leading prayers, singing worship songs and making us laugh was that most of them seemed somehow different. I couldn't understand what it was. I did know that whilst I just loved being there, and felt safe and comfortable, nevertheless, I wasn't really one of them. Whilst I had no difficulty following all that was going on and taking part with genuine enthusiasm, I found it difficult when we got to the 'religious' bits that meant expressing our personal faith. I felt all hot under the collar when people talked about their relationship with God, despite believing in God, I just felt embarrassed when these adults I so respected started talking about knowing Jesus as their Lord and Saviour. Intellectually I understood, but emotionally this was scary stuff and I could understand why people said Christians were weird. Even though I was only eleven, it did concern me that I might be associating with weird people - wasn't I weird enough without any help from others? A few weeks later I was at another similar meeting and this time it felt so completely different - now I was truly at home and now I really understood what these people were talking about. So what had bought about the change?

One Sunday morning I went along as usual to Girl Covenanters, led by Caroline, who I just adored. But despite wanting to be there, as usual I simply couldn't behave myself. I turned up late because I had been captivated by watching vintage cars. Holy Trinity Redhill is on the A23 London to Brighton road where the annual Veteran Car Run passes through. I've no doubt I made a lot of fuss about taking my seat and kept it up for the next half-hour. Eventually their patience was stretched to the limit and one of the leaders suggested that since I clearly did not want to be there it would be best if I just went home. I'm sure I put on a good show of smiling and waving my way out of the door - what did I care? But of course, once on my own, I was back with the emotional struggle of recognising the shame I brought upon myself, knowing that I really did not want to behave like that especially when with people I so liked and respected, and yet also recognising that I was quite incapable of changing myself. And, underlying it all, was the painful awareness that yet again I was being rejected. The despondent belief that no matter where I went I would never truly be wanted. Not wanting to arrive home early since that might mean that I would have to explain that I had been expelled yet again, and that might mean Muriel would say that I didn't need to go any more, I stood for the next half hour at the side of the road waving at the car drivers with tears streaming down my face.

The following week there was no Covenanters since it was Remembrance Sunday, and I had attended church parade with my guide company at another church in town. That afternoon, my parents decided to go for a walk, and most unusually left me home alone. That was an unheard-of experience for me so I intended to make the most of it. But somehow I found myself sitting and thinking through recent events and remonstrating with myself about my behaviour, why couldn't I be good - even when I really wanted to? After all, I had prayed about it, hadn't I? I was remembering a month or two earlier when I had gone back to St Matthew's to return some music, I still sang in the choir regularly even though I had changed schools by now. I had found the church empty and just enjoyed wandering around the peaceful building. I remember looking at some leaflets about overseas missionary work and thinking that perhaps, once I had trained as a nurse, I would be able to do something like that. And then the realisation hit me - who was I kidding - I couldn't get through a single day without being in trouble of some kind, and usually many kinds!

In utter desperation I had cried out to God "I just want to be good - please, make me good" I didn't know it then, but I certainly know now that it would be impossible for God to hear a prayer like that, from one his little ones, and not respond.

So there I was, home alone, and starting to face up to who and what I was. I have absolutely no doubt that as I sat there alone in that room, I found myself in the presence of a mighty God. Suddenly, and with awful clarity, I saw myself as God sees us when we try to live without him. Now you may think that an eleven-year-old child doesn't have much in the way of sin to be aware of. If you do, you are quite wrong. I may not have had much practice in being evil, or any real experience in the ways of the world, but what I discovered was that at the core of my being my nature was just the same as every other human who has ever lived, bar one. Utterly self-centred, wilfully disobedient and rebellious, deceitful, envious, jealous - and the list goes on. Dicken's *Ghost of Christmas Past* was a pale reflection on what the Holy Spirit revealed to me that afternoon, I saw even my best efforts as just contriving; I saw in full technicolour and vivid detail the most terrible sight I have ever seen - the human soul fully revealed in its natural state! Believe me, it's a sight I never want to see again. The prophet Isaiah summed it up perfectly when he said "*All of us have become like one who is unclean, and all our righteous acts are like filthy rags . . .* "

Yet again, I cried out to God from the depths of my soul, "what do I do - help me!" Even as I spoke the horror of what I had just seen left along with the panic - and a sense of calm came over me. I felt God was saying that I had a choice, either I could continue to live my life my way, and be my own boss, or I could hand over the reins of my life completely to Him. I knew there was no place between these two options, and I also instinctively knew that I had to make the decision here and now.

There is one thing that I am certain of, and that is that God created humankind with the ability to make their own decisions; he endowed us with what theologians would call 'free will'. If he hadn't we would have been just automatons, sophisticated robots. If He had made us love Him that just wouldn't be love - merely a programmed instinct. Instead, He took the risk of giving us the choice to accept Him or reject Him. And being both eternal and omnipotent he knew full well what the outcome of that risk would be: that most of his creation would choose the latter and all that came with it, such as the loss of perfection in ourselves and in creation, and eventually the death of His Son as the only way out from the consequences of our bad choices.

So I know that I had a choice in the matter on that Sunday afternoon - that's a theological certainty - but looking back it felt that actually I had no choice. If you've been underwater for some time and you are running out of oxygen, and then suddenly a hand plucks you out of the water - do you keep holding your breath? No, of course not, you gratefully gasp great lungful's of air. Do you turn round and bite the hand that just rescued you and plunge yourself back under the water to drown - or do you to look up at the face of the one who has just saved you? The answer is rhetorical. I took the only option that seemed open to me - I threw myself into the lifeboat.

As God challenged me, and I responded to Him, I literally felt my life change - I knew I had become a new person. When my parents came home, they could tell even then; my mother asked "what's come over you - you seem a different person?" she couldn't have been more right. When I joyfully told them that I'd just become a Christian, her response was "oh that, lots of youngsters go through a religious stage - you'll grow out of it!" She couldn't have been more wrong. Muriel died many years ago, becoming badder and sadder the older she grew; whereas my life has just got better and better.

It was by far the easiest decision I have ever made and one I have never regretted for a second, despite the troubles I have lived through since; and it was also by far the most life changing. Yes, meeting Michael, having our children and grandchildren, were monumental events in my life story - but that decision was the foundation on which everything else was built. I'm just so grateful that God didn't leave me to my own devices for too long and called me out as a child. I'm certain He spared me a great deal of suffering.

Years later when I and James, my younger brother, and Len, my older brother, actually got together for the first time since we were in St Christopher's, I was deeply saddened by something they told me.

After our mother had abandoned him James spent a few years in Skye with his stepfather and half-brothers and then returned to Barkingside to live with her for a short while. It wasn't long before he got himself signed up to the merchant navy. Knowing he had an older brother in Australia he got a berth on a ship going in that direction. Once he arrived in the antipodes he jumped ship and went off in search of his long-lost brother – and amazingly he found him! They told me how they had often gone on long motorbike rides, often worse for wear and always driving at way over the speed limit. Both of them knew how foolish this was, but they both felt that it didn't really matter if they didn't make it back home - since neither of them really had a home. It's easy to wonder why people can make such a mess of their lives with drugs and alcohol abuse, but emotional pain can bring on self-destructive behaviour in a way that physical pain seldom does. Looking from the outside the casual observer would believe that these two young men had everything to live for, yet on the inside, they had nothing - except a lifetime of hurt and rejection, and a wild pain that drove them to excess at every turn. Yes, I too had known that searing and bewildering pain and it was growing greater as I was going through my teens, but as I said, God spared me a great deal, I met Him when I was eleven and Michael when I was sixteen. I have no idea what my life might have been like had I not been so blessed, but I have a strong feeling that it would have been short and very troubled.

This knowledge of "there but for the grace of God go I . . ." has left me very sensitive to the 'naughty child' you find in most groups. The reality, I believe, is not always what people think they see - the desire to show off or just cause trouble. It can often be the silent screaming of a wounded and damaged child working its way out through their behaviour. These are the ones that we should be looking out for and taking under our wing, in just the way a dozen or more good people did for me. They say 'it takes a village to raise a child' well it certainly takes a church family to raise a young Christian and I have so many people to thank for seeing me through those difficult years. Not least was Caroline, my Covenantor leader and her parents. 'The Whalleys' became a surrogate family for me and gave me a wonderful bolthole to escape to. Naturally my parents hated them and would have stopped me spending time with them, but Mr Whalley was well regarded locally and a good friend of the dreaded Revd Bridgeland. Even children from normal, happy homes can benefit from spending time with other families, but for children in difficult circumstances it's often a lifeline.

Now that I was actually listening to what God was saying to me He was able to start sorting out all the wrong responses and attitudes that plagued me. Actually, I'm not sure if even He realised just how long this would take - we're still both working on it!

One of the first tasks was to get out of the habit of lying. I tend to think quickly and could even outclass Muriel who was a consummate liar. Indeed she regularly gave me lessons in the art of lying. We would meet someone in the street and I would do the usual child thing of pretending to be bored and not listening to the conversation when I was actually taking it all in. A while later we would meet someone else and I would listen amazed as the complete opposite of what had just been said was now presented to someone else. On numerous occasions I would be made to practise the next lie she wanted me to present to my father when we got home. We would go shopping and buy some shoes for me and a dress for her perhaps. On the bus home as the price tickets were being removed, I had to rehearse the amounts she wanted him to think she had paid, not what they had actually cost; I think it had become more natural for her to lie than to tell the truth. But if I lied to her, or she even suspected that I was lying, then all hell would break loose; and I don't use that phrase lightly.

****

On the Saturday afternoon before Holiday Club 1966 started the next day, the team members were gathered for a meeting. We were told the two Michael's were coming down from Islington again and might arrive at any time so we started business without them. I remember we were halfway through the opening prayer when the door squeaked open and Michael Wells, and two of the family he was staying with, tried to creep in unnoticed. We were sat in concentric circles and Michael ended up sitting almost opposite to me, and I found myself thinking that I now realised what all the fuss had been about the previous year. Unbeknown to me Michael had no real memory of the little girl who had been part of the team the year before. Now Michael was (and still is) three years older than me. In the general scale of things this is not very significant, but when you are just sixteen and a young man who is nineteen, a university student, and comes from London to boot, appears on your horizon - the gap seems enormous.

So in a time-honoured way I found myself completely losing track of the proceedings and trying to take covert looks at him under my eyelashes. It was odd because every time I looked in his direction I could have sworn that he had been looking in mine and had just turned away as I looked up. Every so often we would mistime the dance and found ourselves caught out by both sneaking a glance at the exact same moment - embarrassing and wonderfully delightful all at the same time.

As is so often the way with these things, the process was helped along by the somewhat clumsy machinations of well-intentioned friends, in this case, Alison and Rosy. I had bought these two along to Holiday club when we all started secondary school together and they had risen up the ranks to junior leader with me. Since they were sitting either side of me they couldn't fail to notice all the covert glances or the fact that when the meeting was over and we were queuing for tea, Michael made a beeline for the three of us. Over the next few days they did that really annoying thing that all good friends do when they see the opportunity to make matches - they kept running off and abandoning me! No sooner did Michael appear on the scene than Rosy remembered she hadn't signed up for lunch, and Alison remembered she had promised to help move equipment, and anyone else who might have been involved in the conversation would be surprised to find themselves manhandled away. It was so wonderfully obvious that we ended up laughing. In fact, we started our relationship with a lot of laughter, and now over half a century on don't suppose we're ever likely to break the habit.

We did what all youngsters do when attracted to each other, we teased each other at every possible opportunity. We had water fights, and mock wrestling matches, and more water fights. Having been soaked a few times I was determined to get my own back. So Alison, Rosy and I set an ambush. We took buckets of water to an upstairs room knowing that Michael would be passing under the window in a few minutes. With the three buckets poised for action I saw him arriving at the allotted spot; as I was about to signal 'target downpour' I suddenly squealed 'stop!' Standing there and looking up at us with a big beam on his face was Michael - wearing my best jumper - which I had imprudently left lying around.

As the week wore in it became increasingly clear that we very much enjoyed each other's company. One evening as I was walking past the church on the way to a youth meeting in someone's house I spotted Michael in the church grounds playing cricket with some of the 'rough boys' from the nearby council estate who had been coming along during the day and seemed to be enjoy themselves. He had been left on his own with them since it was assumed that because he worked with 'rough' London boys, the local boys would be eating out of his hand. This was quite a correct assumption, he has always been able to manage every style and condition of child, and usually just by raising an eyebrow.

I stood at the gate watching him and thinking "just what is this strange thing that has come over me?". A thousand pop songs have put it much more lyrically than that, but you know what I mean. When I finally arrived at the meeting all I could think about was being so disappointed that Michael wasn't going to be there, and then feeling guilty since I knew he was doing something much more valuable by spending his time with the youngsters. Eventually, he did turn up and I tried not to look too excited, especially when he offered to walk me home after the meeting was over. It was on that walk that he told me that he had something important to sort out. What I, and even the

Holy Trinity intelligence network, did not know, was that Michael had a girlfriend back in Islington. He and Jane had been going out for a couple of years. Even as my heart plummeted at the news it started to rise again when he went on to say that, however, the way he was starting to feel about me meant that he couldn't continue like that. If it was alright with me, he said, he would be going back to London by train the next day in order to finish things with Jane so that we would be free to start going out. Well of course it was quite alright with me, though I did just manage to have enough grace to feel sorry for Jane.

A few months later I met Jane when I was visiting London and found her a very gracious and lovely girl. I'm glad to say that she soon found herself a new boyfriend at university and they went on to marry; but I'm also very sad to say that Jane was badly hurt in the Moorgate Tube disaster in 1975, as she was travelling to work. She survived but died a year later from her injuries. Jane had had a very tough childhood, being raised by a single mother who was an alcoholic. From the human perspective, it seems so tragic that she suffered so much in her short life. From God's perspective, Jane is where she was always meant to be - in His presence. In the grand scale of things, a short life or a long life makes very little difference.

Preparing for the Future

Whilst I was growing up in Redhill and my older brother, Len, was being shipped out to Australia: our younger brother James was back with our mother. James was born posthumously and is eleven months younger than me. During this time my mother found herself pregnant again and the father of the child wanting to have nothing to do with the situation. This child, my half-sister Heather, was adopted shortly after birth and none of us has seen her since. Doris did try to make contact with her once but was told quite clearly that she wanted nothing to do with her. I hope and pray that she has had a good life.

Our Mother then went on to marry again; this time it was a fisherman from the Isle of Skye. James went to live with her and his stepfather, and when twin boys appeared on the scene it often fell to young James to look after them. He grew very fond of his younger siblings, which is just as well, since whilst they were still quite small their mother decided to return to Barkingside in East London. I think we have already established that Doris lacked maternal instinct, which becomes all the more evident when you realise that in returning south she failed to take any of the children with her. Poor James was left to be raised by a stepfather and begrudging step-grandmother. He returned to live with his mother in his teens, but not surprisingly, the relationship was never really repaired.

Given that Doris was keen on parties and dancing, hated church and was not at all interested in the countryside, it's not surprising that she couldn't cope for long living in a tight knit, somewhat dour, presbyterian community, as it was back then. I once met the twins when they were in their early twenties but never really got to know them. Roddie had become a squaddie in the British Army. On 27 August, the day Lord Mountbatten was assassinated, he witnessed some of his mates blown to pieces in front of him at the Warrenpoint massacre. He never fully recovered from the experience and later took his own life. His brother, Donnie, has suffered from mental illness for most of his adult life and has been institutionalised for a great part of it. It's hard not to apportion blame for such blighted lives, but it's impossible to know if these things might have happened anyway. After all, there are plenty of children raised in loving, secure environments, whose difficult adult lives bear no reflection on their upbringing; the converse must also be true. But such philosophising cannot ameliorate the pain and loss my siblings suffered.

Meanwhile, far away in Australia, Len was having his early years shaped by misfortune. It's sad to say that Great Britain is the only country to have given away thousands of its children, and for so many of those children like Len, they led a life that has been described by many as one of 'slave labour'. Yes, they were fed, but not terribly well, and clothed, but barely and badly. If a youngster in Britain worked on his parent's farm he might not get paid but he would never have to work the long gruelling hours, week in week out, for years on end without any reward; and in any case, he probably stood to inherit the farm one day. But when Len left the Fairbridge farm he had just a few dollars and a change of clothes. In his own words:

I joined the railway and worked in small towns such as Narromine and Coonamble in NSW and eventually joined a pop group in the country city of Orange. A year or so later I went to Sydney and joined another group called the Cavemen as their lead singer.

After a mad whirlwind season of drugs and rock and roll, in 1968 I thought that if I could find my mother who I hadn't seen for 14 years, I would discover who I really was. It wasn't to be so. I travelled to the Northern Territory and worked for 7 months to earn enough money to travel back to England. I did the 'hippy trail' up to Singapore, India and Kathmandu. With long hair, a dilly bag and a flute I couldn't play I wandered through Northern Asia until in October 1968, after what seemed like years on the road, I arrived in England and came face to face with my mother!

Meanwhile, back in the UK, I was beating him to it.

Towards the end of that incredible week, I found myself sitting with Michael on the doorstep of the church hall, talking as only two people falling in love can. When he asked about my 'real' family the floodgates opened and it all poured out. He produced a freshly laundered, neatly folded handkerchief from his pocket, and passed it over to help stem the tears - the first of many such handkerchiefs. I didn't really know about James then, but I did know I had an older brother called Len, and that he had been sent to Australia. I remember learning in a history lesson in junior school that we had sent our convicts to Australia in the past to get rid of them, and it had occurred to me that perhaps Len had been naughty and was some kind of child prisoner. Not far from the truth perhaps.

When I told Michael about Len I felt I was taking a risk revealing what a strange background I came from, yet I somehow knew that he would take it in his stride, as indeed he did. He didn't think that my hopes and prayers to meet Len someday were ridiculous, and his reaction left me comforted and calmed, though had I known how this was all going to come about I would have felt anything but calm!

Later that day I took some time out and went and sat on my own in the empty church, ignoring the happy noise of fun and games going on outside. You probably know the old joke: "How do you make God laugh?" answer "Tell Him your plans!"

I was now sixteen and pretty certain what I wanted to do with my life. As soon as I was legally old enough I was going to sign up to the Queen Alexander's Nursing Corps. I had wanted to be a nurse for as long as I can remember and was also fascinated by the military. An example of this was my obsession with Lawrence of Arabia. It began with that wonderful film of his life starring Peter O'Toole and Omar Sharif. Anyone who has ever seen the film remembers that long opening with the speck on the horizon of the shimmering desert, and the absolute silence until you start to realise that you are hearing the bells on a camel bridle coming towards you. I knew next to nothing about the subject, and I was only thirteen at the time, but somehow I managed to gain entrance to the Odeon Cinema and watched utterly spellbound. I came out of the cinema two hours later riding my camel all the way home, watching out for Turkish soldiers hidden in the wadies I passed through.

As I've mentioned my parents didn't really read and so we had very few books. Michael and I live surrounded by books, and at the last count we had over two thousand, but in those days the local library was my only source. In an amazing coincidence, shortly after meeting *Al-Aurens* I was dusting through the house, one of my weekend chores that usually went on for most of Saturday. This meant moving the ten or so books kept between two bookends on the chest of drawers that no one ever looked at, but this time I actually looked at them. Two of them appeared to be identical and turned out to be the two volumes of Lawrence's memoirs *The Seven Pillars of Wisdom*. By the time I had read the poem of dedication on the first page:

> *I loved you, so I drew these tides of*
> *Men into my hands*
> *And wrote my will across the*
> *Sky in stars*
> *To earn you freedom, the seven*
> *Pillared worthy house,*
> *That your eyes might be*
> *Shining for me*
> *When I came*

. . . I was in love with the man, the myth and the book.

My father was somewhat surprised when I asked if I could read them. Since I wasn't going to explain that I had been to the pictures on my own and without permission, I had to do some quick thinking and explained that we were studying the First World War at school. He said I was welcome to them since he found them too boring to read. Over the next few years I read both volumes from cover to cover three times. At the end of every summer term in secondary school (a Church of England girl's school), we were asked to choose a 'summer project' to work on through the holiday, on a subject we were interested in, ready to bring back at the beginning of the next school year. I suppose it was a kind of competition, with most people returning three or four pages with lots of pictures on 'where I went for my holiday' or 'grooming my horse'. So my first project was a small book on how Lawrence trained up the Arabs for guerrilla warfare, and the following year it was on the Battle of Aqaba. I think the year after that I tackled the betrayal of Lawrence and the Arabs in the peace conferences following the war - not that I really understood the politics of it but I felt strongly that he had been cheated. I actually won a prize after that one - a book token and a certificate for 'Persistence'.

The 'nature versus nurture' argument fascinates me since, not having grown up with my family, and having no knowledge of them, I could not have been influenced by them in the nurture stage, but now that I have met my family and found out more about my background I have discovered so many similarities and preferences that can only be explained by a shared gene-pool. So whilst I was making plans to be a military nurse I had no knowledge that my Great Aunt had been matron of a large hospital in Belfast and that my Great Uncle Paddy had been a founder of the SAS, whose training techniques are used in special forces to this day.

Another coincidence supporting the nature/shared genes argument was my choice of sport. In my late teens I discovered trampolining, a sport that I continued into my early 30s until the onset of Sjögren's Syndrome. I enjoyed it so much that I trained as a coach up to senior level and also trained as a competition judge, sometimes judging at international competitions. But Len, on the other side of the world, probably discovered the sport first. He had won a scholarship to the district high school, which meant he lived away from the farm throughout the week for a few years. Whilst there he became a champion in the schools high-diving league and they used a trampoline for training purposes, so he became highly skilled in performing multiple twisting somersaults. We are both naturally very competitive so when, years later, I took him along to the sports centre where I ran a trampoline club, the competition to outdo each other was fierce - think of *Westside Story* and the dance-off between the Jets and the Sharks - you get the picture. It was a wonder we both made it home in one piece.

But now all these dreams and plans of nursing and the military life seemed to be more of a problem than a joy. The idea of marriage had simply never entered my thinking, even the idea of a boyfriend had not been seriously considered since in our church youth group we had it made quite clear to us that the reason for having such a relationship was because it might, eventually, lead to marriage. So you didn't go out with someone if you didn't consider them a potential life partner. Simples. It all seems so much more complicated these days!

As I sat there in that peaceful building I kept trying to unravel this Gordian Knot. I had set my sites on being a career nurse and rising through the ranks of the army; there was simply no room for long term relationships; and yet, my heart was telling me in no uncertain terms that this young man I had just met was the person I wanted to spend the rest of my life with, and that life without him was even more inconceivable that giving up my dreams. I also had to consider if this was just me being a year later than the other girls in having 'a thing' about Michael Wells - did he feel the way I did or perhaps just see me as a silly little girl? Despite having absolutely no experience of life or relationships, I just somehow knew that our attraction was mutual, and I had already picked up that Michael was not the sort of person to take such things lightly.

Eventually, it dawned on me that the purpose of taking this time out was so that I could pray about the situation, how else was I to know if this rapidly blooming relationship was part of God's plan for my life. So I sat and poured it all out, and then, being the impatient creature that I am, I wanted an answer - and now if you don't mind, before lunchtime, please!

I was always taught that God often speaks through the scriptures, but that this should always be a part of a daily discipline of prayer and Bible reading, and that the Bible was not to be treated as a magic book of instant answers. Despite knowing this in my head, my heart suggested that God would indeed speak to me right now through His Word; and so I picked up the nearest Bible in the pew I was sitting in, turned it over a few times praying along the lines of "please tell me if I'm to let go of one set of dreams and start on another that my heart seems to be leading me to". I closed my eyes, rotated and flipped open the book and stuck my finger on the page. When I opened my eyes the writing was the right way up and my index finger had landed squarely on verse 9 in Mark chapter 10:

What therefore God hath joined together, let not man put asunder.

Being somewhat shocked by what I saw I repeated the procedure - this time my finger landed on the words:

Jesus said, Go and do likewise

Now I was truly shocked and amazed, and a tad scared, I blurted out "Lord am I making this up or is it from you?" So I closed my eyes one last time and twirled the book around in my hands before opening it - plonking my finger down hard on the page and then opening my eyes to see:

Oh, you of little faith!

Of course, now that I am older and wiser I would most certainly not recommend that as a way to behave. But as we have learned from our forays into the Land of Narnia "Aslan is not a tame lion", and he sometimes meets the need at the time in ways that the more circumspect of His followers might consider somewhat wild. I left that building in a welter of emotion, but quite certain that God had a deep interest in what was going on in my life and was leading me forward to times I could not begin to imagine.

Michael and I become engaged about three weeks after that glorious Holiday Club. We had the sense not to share this arrangement with anyone at that stage, since we knew folk would think we were far too young for such a commitment and anyway, we barely knew each other! All true of course, but somehow we just knew this was part of God's plan for us.

Life at the Seaside

When I moved with my parents to Eastbourne in the autumn of 1966, having just left school, and met Michael that summer, I signed up to attend the local tertiary college to see if I could improve on my rather dismal exam results. At first I was not allowed to do this full-time and was instructed to get a job to earn my keep. I discovered that since my father had been a serving soldier, when he died his widow and children each received an army pension, and as he had paid extra it was a reasonable monthly income. Whilst I was in Barnardo's they received it, but as soon as I was fostered by the Peter's it came with me. Naturally, they considered this money was theirs by right and not a penny of it was put by for my future. Had they been living on a low income I could have understood that it was helping to put food on the table; but being a master printer my father was very well paid, in those days he would have earned more than a teacher.

One major problem throughout our marriage has been housing, and I often had to struggle not to be bitter when I considered that even if they had saved only half of that pension over the years, it would have been enough to help with a deposit for a house. However when they discovered that, if I went to college full-time the pension was safe - so they grudgingly allowed me to spend one more year in education.

One freedom that I had established after the move to Eastbourne, despite my parents' absolute annoyance, was that I would travel up to London every other weekend to stay with Michael's family and on alternative weekends Michael would come to Eastbourne. Of course, it was too much to expect to be able to spend any of my earnings on train fare; sometimes I would manage to save enough in two weeks out of the pocket money I was allowed to keep, and if I hadn't Michael had usually given me enough to cover the fare should I need it. He also bought me clothes, study books etc and paid for all our outings. He was training as a teacher at Goldsmiths College, University of London. These were the golden years for student grants, and since he was living at home with his parents he had little in the way of expenses other than his train fares and other travel. I suspect that much of his income went to supporting me, keeping me in essentials. Though we did spend money on luxuries, like bags of chips as we walked home after a nighttime stroll along the seafront at Eastbourne. One of the treats we allowed ourselves was coffee in the Lyons Tea Shop in Terminus Road where I daringly drank milk with a dash; a very weak coffee, probably an early version of the now fashionable latte.

One of the friends I made at college was Charlotte, the daughter of an English ambassador, whose family had just returned to the UK. The first time I was invited to tea it was a sunny afternoon and Pater Familias suggested we sit outside in the garden. Chas, Griselda and I dragged three rather dilapidated deckchairs out of the stable block, set them up and plonked ourselves onto them at just about the same time. At which point all three chairs were rent asunder and the three of us ended up flat on our backs with the deckchair frames wrapped around us. Sir Anthony laughed so much we thought he might have a heart attack. When he finally recovered he wheezed "well those were being used by my family before the Titanic sank - so I suppose they've lasted well considering!"

Michael and I took many long walks on, over, and around the South Downs during my two years in Eastbourne, but sometimes I visited Beachy Head with my friends Chas and Grizelda. One afternoon Grizelda and I were playing silly games while Chas dozed in the sun. Grizelda turned round to shout something just in time to see me leap over the edge of the cliff. At least that was what she thought she was seeing, in fact, I was close to the edge and could see a large promontory of cliff extending about six or seven feet below the visible edge - quite big enough to accommodate at least half a dozen people - so in my crazy way I jumped down just to get another view. Chas was rudely awakened by the ear-piercing screams of Grizelda who was convinced she had just seen her friend jump to her death. Having been alerted to the fact that I'd probably got something wrong I was now trying to work out how to get back up that little cliff face that was taller than me. When I looked up at the completely white faces of two totally shocked people I realised that it was very gracious of them to offer to help me back to the land of the living.

When we first formed our trio they of course wanted to know if I had a boyfriend. I proceeded to tell them about Michael, who was at university in London, and who came down to Eastbourne every other weekend. "Really" was their general response. For a few weeks I would tell them on Monday morning about my weekend in London or Michael's visit to Eastbourne. Despite the fact that I spent a lot of time wearing his university scarf and had a photo of him, I think they were both convinced that he was just a figment of my imagination.

Then one, Friday they casually asked if Michael was coming down for the weekend, on hearing the affirmative they, even more casually, asked what time the train arrived. So I wasn't unduly surprised when, having met Michael from the train and we were walking across the station concourse, we bumped into the two of them who just happened to be walking home that way! I couldn't really be too surprised at their amazement over this relationship since I was equally amazed - and I was living it.

I managed to scrape through a few more qualifications, getting really a good grade for English Literature; and this was solely due to the encouragement of one kind teacher who took it upon herself to care. I don't remember her name but I do remember that she was recently widowed and had a severely disabled child, so life must have been tough for her. I taught for many years in FE colleges and know how disheartening it can be struggling with many of the teenagers you work with. The adults are usually there because they want to be and can be a great pleasure to teach, but a lot of the youngsters really don't want to be there. I only taught IT, but I imagine English Literature was not a subject many of her students were passionate about. Certainly, for the first few weeks at least, it must have been really hard going for her. But I loved the way she explained the background to poems and books, and before long I was staying after class to ask questions and talk about the books she had bought from home to help me study. Because she believed in me, I believed in myself, and was able to do better than I ever expected. Thank goodness for lovely people like her who are able to enthuse and encourage even the less likely students.

We had been going steady for over six months when we decided to make our engagement official. Michael was staying for the weekend and on the Saturday morning he asked my father for permission to marry me. I imagine by that stage they had already given up on the idea of chaining me to them for life, and I also suspect they were just a little wary of Michael. He was educated, well spoken, and had a sort of authority that brooked no interference. Tom reluctantly agreed, and that morning we went into town to buy an engagement ring. We went into Charlwood's the Jeweller in Langney Road, where Michael spent an awesome thirteen pounds ten shillings on a little ring, that I wore home. There is a faded photograph taken that day of me overlooking the beach and wearing a yellow skirt and jacket. That and the ring itself are the only mementoes of that day. There was no party, and I suspect very few cards, if any. We simply got engaged, no advance announcement. We did however get one engagement present, a set of four wooden handled steak knives and forks from Michael's mother, they are still in regular use.

There I was, barely seventeen years old and engaged to be married. Looking back it is possible that my adopted parent still hoped that they could find a way of persuading us to care for them, there was even some talk of letting us live with them. At that stage Michael knew of my adoption and of some of the domestic tensions; I had told him about Len in Australia, but he knew nothing of my childhood experiences of violence and abuse. Not only was I wary of opening up too much, but I still felt that nobody would believe me and felt quite sure that it was only a matter of time before the love of my life would abandon me - after all everybody else had.

That afternoon we played tennis, where yet again I demonstrated my superiority on the court - it's not often I beat Michael in anything but I do enjoy trying. From then on I took to stirring my coffee with the spoon in my left hand, hoping that the glint of a tiny diamond might be noticed.

Our weekends together quickly developed their own routine. One week I would catch the train after work on Friday arriving at London Victoria in the early evening where Michael would meet me and we would catch the bus to Islington where he lived with his parents. We would spend Saturday and Sunday together and I would catch the last train home on Sunday evening.

One Friday afternoon, in the middle of winter I, along with the rest of the Tax Office staff were sent home mid-afternoon due to a severe weather warning on the south coast. Knowing that a number of people in our office travelled some distance we were told to make our way home as soon as possible. Now if I had been a sensible young person, I would have recognised that it was not a good idea to head off for London, even if it was earlier than usual; however, when it came to being with Michael I didn't have a sensible thought in my head, and so set off to the station to catch the next train. It would seem that a lot of other people were sent home as every carriage was packed and I was lucky to get a seat. The snowstorm had already started as we were boarding the train, when we were about thirty minutes into the journey it became obvious that we had slowed to about walking pace. Just as the driver was starting to make an announcement he was abruptly cut off, as the engine stopped and the lights went out. When the poor beleaguered man finally got to our carriage he explained, for the umpteenth time, that the rather elderly rolling stock we were currently occupying simply hadn't been able to cope with the effort and the engine had completely seized up, thus no lighting or heating.

Despite it being dark and cold we had been having a rather fun time down our end of the train, all sitting close together with any spare clothing we had about us being spread across our knees, and cheering each other up with jokes and stories. We were told another train would be coming to fetch us in half an hour or so. It was actually another two hours before not one, but two trains arrived. One had come up from Eastbourne and was parked behind us, so that those wanting to give up and go back had only to walk the length of the train, get out of the end carriage and climb up into the waiting train. Whereas those hardy souls who wanted to carry on into the face of the blizzard were required to leave the train and walk ten minutes up the track to where the rescue train was parked in a siding. So I decided to do the sensible thing and take the train back home. Yeah right! I'm kidding of course.

I remember feeling that I was already frozen solid before leaving the train, I was dressed for work not mountaineering, wearing a lightweight coat, a short crimplene dress, thin tights and some very neat little strappy shoes. Feeling like I had wandered onto the film-set of Scot of the Antarctic, I set off following about twenty other mad people leaning into the blizzard and wading through the snow, dragging my little case with me. I knew next to nothing about hypothermia at that stage, but looking back I now know that I was well into the first stage, when I suddenly realised that a group of superheroes had come looming through the mist to find us, since it was well over twenty minutes since we had set off. Finally we were helped up into a proper train with lights and heating, and blankets and hot drinks all round. This train finally got us to Victoria station very late in the evening, about seven hours after we had set off, where a slightly frantic Michael had been pacing the platform for hours. I stayed an extra night in London and got safely home on the Monday evening. When I went into the Office on Tuesday people we asking about the 'terrible' weekend I must have had. Actually, whilst I didn't enjoy the experience of being semi-frozen, I still thought it had been a great weekend. It's amazing how love changes your perspective on things.

Every other weekend Michael would travel down to Eastbourne on the Friday and head back to London on Sunday. Invariably, whatever the weather, we would stay out of the house as much as possible. In the colder months we might wander around the shopping centre in the morning, and then walk along the seafront during the afternoon, and even in the evenings. During the summer we would walk over the Downs, perhaps catching the open topped bus to Beachy Head. Over a series of weekends we walked as far as Newhaven, catching the bus part way. One of Michael's favourite walks was from Exeat farm along the course of the Cuckmere River to the sea. We might walk on the beach, and even risked swimming sometimes. One day we even walked along the seashore from Eastbourne to Birling gap under the towering cliffs of Beachy Head, a very risky walk at the best of times.

Thus two happy years passed filled with a lot of fun and a lot of yearning. Cliff Richard's *Visions of You* and *Miss You Nights* became my most played records, and I can't hear those songs, even now, without getting a lump in my throat. Since talking on the phone wasn't easy, and neither of us really enjoyed it anyway, we made the most of the social media of the day - pen and ink! I think it's fair to say that Michael wrote almost every day we were apart and I would get a letter from him on an almost daily basis. Tucked away in our attic is a large cardboard box full of hundreds of those letters - mine were less frequent than Michael's but I did my bit. It became a standing joke with the postman who often arrived just as I heading off on my bike to work. If he had a letter he would pop it into the basket on the front of my bicycle saying "see, he still loves you". But sometimes the letter came in the second post and Mr Postman would laughingly pronounce "sorry, seems he doesn't love you anymore". I laughed along with him at the joke; nevertheless, such a day would seem to go on forever whilst I watched the clock - longing to get home and find my letter. Which I did, sitting waiting for me on the hall table - unopened - without even any sign of it having been steamed open and resealed. So how did this change come about?

When I first arrived in Eastbourne I started to attend Holy Trinity and very quickly made friends with the curate's two daughters who were around my age. I was always made welcome in their home, and although they were undoubtedly worried about my being engaged at such a young age, they never made me feel awkward or questioned me about it. I think they soon sensed that things weren't quite right at home and sometimes asked me a few searching questions, but for all the reasons already covered I couldn't bring myself to ask for help. Besides, the physical cruelty had mostly stopped now and it was just basically a constant war of attrition, and since I'd never really known anything else I could cope. Or so I thought, until one Saturday morning, one of those rare weekends when Michael and I were apart, when things got out of hand. A letter had arrived for me which I caught them opening. I complained, who wouldn't, and immediately world war III broke out. They told me in many and varied ways how they hated me and wished they had never set eyes on me. Had I been staying out late, doing drink and drugs etc I might have understood why I was such a problem, but I didn't have time for any of those things. I split my time between Michael, work, church and the occasional game of tennis. What was so terrible about that? But of course, it was terrible from their perspective since, being the ungrateful child that I was, I was planning to marry quite soon and leave them in the lurch. Leaving them with no nursemaid in their old age, which was fast advancing.

I'm not sure why I found this particular attack so unbearable since, as I said, they had mainly stopped the physical abuse, and I had certainly been on the receiving end of far worse, but the intensity and ferociousness was so great that it just broke me, and when the pushing and shoving started something in me snapped. In a flash it dawned on me, I was reaching adulthood and I no longer needed to accept this kind of abuse. Having established that in my own mind I grabbed my bag and left the house telling them that I would only be returning to collect my things.

I love the story of our friend's daughter who often ran away as a child, but when she got to the bottom of their road she knew she wasn't allowed to cross the main road on her own, so she just turned around and went home again.

Well that particular child hadn't even been born when I fled the house, but when I got to the bottom of the road (I'd been in such a hurry that I hadn't even taken my bicycle) I crossed the road and kept going to the other side of town, to Holy Trinity - sanctuary! As I walked those few miles I was finally able to face up to what I had always known, certainly since Nanny had died anyway, I was the object of an unrealistic plan that had just never worked. We had never achieved family and never could, and despite the sense of freedom now I knew that I didn't have to endure that existence anymore, there was still a deep sense of bereavement; not for what I was losing, but rather for what I had never had.

I sat down in a corner of the church, just asking God to tell me what to do next. I didn't have a clue; I'd jumped out of the boat without a lifebelt but I was determinedly swimming away from the boat with no thought of return. Suddenly I realised that someone was talking to me and asking me if I was alright. It was Ivor Reith, the curate and my friend's father, who could clearly see that I was far from alright. At least he only had to get this sobbing heap over the road to their house opposite the church. The girls were away so Mr & Mrs Reith were able to sit down and gradually work out what I was telling them. Some of the looks that passed between them made me start to think "there, I knew it, they don't believe me - why would they?" But it was too late, the floodgates had finally opened and no force of nature could close them again. When I finally calmed down and was being restored with tea and cake, Ivor announced that he was just popping across the road to see the vicar, the Revd Frederick Kerr-Dineen. I barely knew the Kerr-Dineens but later I was to learn that he had also been adopted as a child, albeit under far different circumstances. Perhaps this is why he took the whole thing very seriously. He contacted his mother who drove over from her home a few miles away to fetch me from the Reith's and took me to spend the day with her. I remember very little about the day other than the wonderful peace of spending time with someone who treated you with respect and kindness. After a lovely supper, which I now had recovered sufficiently enough to do justice to, Revd Kerr-Dineen collected me and took me back to the Reith's. As the four of us sat down in overstuffed armchairs I was panicking again; I felt like I had felt so often standing outside the head-teacher's office awaiting the verdict over yet another misdemeanour.

Ivor explained that he and Revd Kerr-Dineen had visited my parents whilst I had been visiting out of town, not once but twice. It appeared that they had not been well received the first time and so had gone off to make some phone calls and take some 'legal advice' as they put it. By this stage I knew my lack of caution in revealing all had been my downfall; not only had I made a complete fool of myself but I was now about to be arrested. But what Ivor said next shocked me to the core - I had never heard anything like it in my life before! He simply said "We believe every word you have told us". If I had been wrongfully arrested and locked up for seventeen years, and was now suddenly being released. I doubt if I could have felt any more amazed and relieved than I did in that moment.

Apparently, armed with 'legal advice' they had returned to the Peter's and told them that they would ask me to return home, and if I chose to do so it would be under the terms that they must agree to and that I would also be aware of. Namely, no more physical or verbal abuse, no more threats and no more opening my mail, they would be checking with me on a weekly basis to see that I was being treated properly. I was also to have my own door key and be allowed to come and go as I pleased. (I don't think I had mentioned that my all my income was taken off me, so it wasn't in the contract and they carried on with that one.) If I chose not to return they would work with the local services and find me somewhere to live, and if I did return and the abuse started again then I would be removed immediately.

We spent some time discussing the pros and cons of my leaving home, and I knew that they would keep their word in finding me alternative accommodation. Nevertheless, I realised as they explained it to me, that since I was not yet legally of age, the Peter's could make things very difficult for my short-term future. Knowing Michael, Ivor and Freddy knew that when we married in a year or so that I would be in safe hands, and that young though we were we seemed to know what we were doing; so it might be better if I returned home and waited out the time.

I reluctantly agreed and Ivor drove me home late that evening, knocking on the front door himself. Muriel opened it with a 'butter wouldn't melt in the mouth' look, which turned quite sheepish when Ivor just gave her a steely look and said, 'Lesley will need a door key by Tuesday so that she can let herself in after she has been to supper with us. Good night!'

Thus began a strange year where I felt rather like a lodger who was paying somewhat over the odds. We barely spoke and I managed to keep out of their way. It was rather odd when Michael arrived to stay every other weekend, since Muriel was all sweetness and light. But she had made the mistake of coming out with a few whopping and ridiculous lies which of course put him on guard; it also mystified him since he came from such a straightforward family.

Leaving the Past Behind

Shortly after we had moved to Eastbourne I had seen an advert in the local paper for a trainee nursery teacher in a local private nursery. Since I liked children this seemed ideal, I applied and was invited for an interview. I got on really well with the head of the nursery and after having been observed leading some games and feeding some of the children, she said "I'm so impressed I'm not going to interview any more of the candidates. Can you start next week, and can you fill in this application to start the training course at the local college?" This I duly did and went home delighted to report that I now had a full-time job that could be fitted around my studies. The first and only question about this new post was "how much are they paying you?" I confessed to not having any idea, "well ring them up and ask" I was told. Not having the first idea about money (still not much improved) I relayed what I was told, which had sounded good to my ears. "That's not enough" was the response "ring them again and tell them you've decided not to take the job." I still remember the pain of that, had I been allowed to make the call on my own I would probably have said something along the lines "my parents have decided that I shouldn't take the job" that would have been hard enough, but I had Muriel standing next to me having just issued the instruction that I was only to say "I'm sorry but I can't take the job". Understandably my erstwhile employer was both disappointed and annoyed with me. I prayed that I wouldn't bump into her again since I would never be able to look her in the eye.

Following that disappointment, I got a full-time job as a clerical assistant with the Inland Revenue in the local Tax

Office, where, fortunately, I was allowed time out to attend college classes. I stayed with them with up until we married in 1968 and a few of my colleagues, who had become friends, travelled up to London to the wedding. By that stage I was paid monthly, but cash was still the usual thing, especially for juniors. As before I had to handover the unopened wage packet, I was actually never quite sure how much I earned. In return I would be given a small amount of money as 'pocket money' and that quite literally was all it was. I didn't need fares since I had been allowed to purchase a second-hand bike out of my earnings and cycled in and out of town every day. And I didn't need to buy food since I was provided with a somewhat dismal sandwich each day (it had crossed my notice that Muriel's adored pet poodle regularly had butcher's steak and minced liver, while I had a luncheon meat sandwich for lunch and egg and chips for supper) – so what did I need money for?

On the London weekends we attend Holy Trinity Islington where Michael's parents had worshipped for many years and where he grew up, both in years and faith. I had already become part of this church family and felt quite at home there, but even so, I was amazed at how generous these dear people were. When Michael mentioned to his friend's mother that we would be getting married in Islington and would like to have the reception in the church hall the wheels were set in motion. He gave the 'ladies' of the church a modest amount for the food, and they laid on a splendid banquet which more than adequately fed half the church congregation, plus a small coach load of folk from Holy Trinity Redhill who had been following our progress, and a small party from Eastbourne; getting on for well over a hundred people. Had we hired caterers we might have just managed a party of ten. The only comparatively small contingent was my own family, that party consisted of my parents who turned up late and my foster sister Christine, who was a bridesmaid along with my two old friends Alison and Rosie.

Everything to do with the church service appeared to come free, even the bell ringing! Michael's mother, Violet, made my dress and the three bridesmaids' dresses, knowing that I could never manage that myself, and Michael had paid for the catering, the cars and all the other incidentals. The only thing left was the flowers, which I said I would pay for.

Our wedding day was set for 10 August 1968. At the end of July I was given two wage packages at work, one for July and one for the two weeks I would be working in August, plus two weeks holiday I was owed. When I handed the July wages over at home I was asked "where's the rest - you owe us a month's rent for August" - "But I'm only here for two weeks" I remonstrated "and I've set that money aside for the wedding flowers. "That's too bad" I was told, "hand it over". Michael, bless him, took it in his stride when I rang him in floods of tears telling him there wouldn't be any flowers. "Don't worry" he calmly said "I'll see to it". And that's just what he did, and has kept on doing through the years.

Another abuse that had finally ceased was the physical abuse and beatings. I think I was about fifteen when, yet again I suddenly found myself under attack for no good reason and having blow after blow rained upon me. Nothing unusual but when I got a resounding blow on the side of my head that made my ears ring, something snapped inside me and I found myself thinking "enough is enough - this has got to stop". So without really thinking about it I planted my feet firmly and swiped the back of my hand sharply across Muriel's face. I've never been tall, but I was a gymnast in training at the time, and quite strong. The look of abject shock that registered on Muriel's face was extraordinary to behold. I don't suppose anyone else had ever given her as good as they got. But I wasn't finished. I drew myself up to my full almost five foot and with a tone of authority that only justified outrage can endow, I rounded on her with a wagging finger saying "if you *ever* lay a hand on me again I'm going straight to the police to report you!". I'm sure it will be no surprise to hear that she never struck me again.

It saddens me that I was driven to such lengths to protect myself, especially since I knew one of God's key commands to all of us is to honour our parents; so I was deeply ashamed of what I had done, and remain so. But I also know that God sees the whole picture, and whilst He would not have suggested such a course of action, neither do I think He would condemn me for protecting myself.

My coming of age was rather peculiar, since I'm one of that select group of Brits born within a certain three-year period – it was a moveable feast. On my eighteenth birthday I did not gain adult status, that was still fixed at twenty-one. But we did know that there was a parliamentary movement in process intended to reduce the age of majority to eighteen; it didn't actually happen until the first day of January 1970, by which time I was coming up to my twentieth birthday. So my eighteenth birthday didn't count for much and by the time I reached twenty-one that wasn't particularly notable either.

By my eighteenth birthday we had been going out for two years and Michael was about to finish college and start teaching when we announced our engagement at Easter of that year and set the date for that summer. My brother-in-law elect, George, kindly hired or borrowed a van and drove Michael from London to collect me from Eastbourne a couple of days before the wedding. I stayed with Michael's parents while he went off to stay with a friend. The wedding was a wonderful occasion and one of the happiest days of my life. There was one person who had asked to be there, but to whom I had to say no, and that was my mother, Doris. So how come the mother who had given me away was wanting to attend our wedding?

****

A year or so before I left home I made a startling discovery. Since my father had retired and we had moved to Eastbourne they had started to run a B&B during the summer, I had to move from room to room to accommodate guests. Whilst trying to make room for my things in a tiny box room I knocked an old suitcase of letters and papers onto the floor. Whilst gathering them back into the case I noticed a letter addressed to my parents with the postmark Barkingside. I knew this was in Essex and I was puzzled about who they might know from that part of the country. I should say, yes, it was nosey of me to read the letter, but generally I had little or no interest in my parent's affairs, so I have no idea why this particular letter attracted my attention - other than the obvious conclusion that I was meant to see it!

It turned out to be a letter from my mother, Doris, written two or so years earlier. Knowing that I was now in my mid-teens and that they were not a young couple, she had written to Barnardo's asking them to forward this letter to my parents, which they duly did. Basically, she was saying that she would love to meet me again, and should I ever need a home, she was now in a position to offer me one. Not surprisingly the letter had never been mentioned to me, which I quite understand - family structures were less fluid then than they are today, and adoption was all very secretive since it often meant that some kind of "shame" was involved. For so long I had dreamed about my mother coming to find me and take me away from my misery - well that was just a childish dream, but now at least I knew she had remembered me. On the odd occasion I dared to ask my parents about my mother I was told that she had never wanted me in the first place and would certainly have forgotten me by now.

It is deeply wounding for anyone of any age to be told they aren't wanted, but for a child, it is just soul-destroying. So often when my parents were arguing, which was quite often, they would end up standing at the bottom of the stairs - knowing I could hear every word in my bedroom. The script would generally go along the lines of - Thomas: "This is all the fault of that child - I told you I didn't want another child at my age but you wouldn't listen!" Muriel: "Well I don't want her now either, pity we can't send her back." What a tragedy for all of us since I didn't want to be with them either. If I could have packed my bag and taken myself back to St Christopher's I would have done it in a trice - although leaving Nanny and the dog would have been hard.

So on reading this letter I copied the name (my mother had remarried) and the address and put the letter back where I'd found it. I already knew that since my mother couldn't find me I was going to have to use that information to find her.

I also knew that I should be sharing this with Michael - we shared everything else - but for reasons I still don't understand I just felt that I should do this alone. I guess that I was probably afraid that people would try to stop me and I didn't dare take that risk. So within a week or so of finding the letter, I took a day's leave from work and told my parents I would be home late as I was meeting friends. I somehow managed to get myself up to London on the train, across to Barking on the underground and then found the address from the letter. Imagine standing on a doorstop knocking on the door waiting to see the person you had been longing to see for over a decade. Now imagine the disappointment when a woman opens the door and you proudly introduce yourself only to hear her say "Sorry love, I'm not Doris, she moved a year ago!" Fortunately, she had only moved a few streets away and I was given directions.

So again I stood on the doorstep waiting to meet my mother - knowing that even if it was her this time I certainly wouldn't recognise her; and I certainly didn't recognise the woman who answered this door. Before I had the chance to say anything she smiled at me and said "oh, I'm sorry, Jim is away working and won't be back for a while. Since I knew I had a younger brother called James, or Jim, I was clearly at the right place but had just been mistaken for one of my brother's friends. "Sorry" I said "but I think it's you I'm looking for - don't you recognise me?" Rather a silly question really since I was a child of seven the last time she had laid eyes on me, and now I was seventeen. For a few seconds she just looked bemused, and then a whole tranche of emotions swept across her face. Poor Doris, she just crumpled before my eyes "It's Dorothy isn't it?" "Yes" I said "well, actually I'm Lesley now."

Despite her lack of maternal instinct my mother had always kept wondering about how I was doing, and always hoped that one day she would see me again. What followed was a very strange day. Doris was just off to her job as a messenger for British Rail at Paddington Station, and she insisted that I came with her. Back on the underground and we travelled on her pass into London. This was long before email and her job was to collect messages and documents from any office or department that requested it and to deliver the goods either to the internal post room or to the various other offices dotted around the station. I can tell you that Paddington, probably like most London stations, is a veritable warren of hidden corridors and underground tunnels. So back and forth we trotted, and in between all the collecting and delivering we carefully began to unravel our strange past. My mother was in tears most of the time and I probably wasn't far behind her. Almost every room we entered the staff would greet her in a friendly way and invariably asked "so who's this?" probably thinking I was a new trainee, and each time Doris proudly answered "it's my daughter!" Since she had worked in that role for about ten years most of them were somewhat bemused and blurted out something like "well I didn't know you had a daughter" to which my mother responded, "well I do and now I've found her". Each time I silently added to the conversation "well actually it was me that did the finding!"

When we visited the office on the top floor, I was told that this was where the senior managers worked. That was fairly obvious when the surroundings became more and more plush. Fast forward two decades when I worked for some years as a national verifier and assessor for City and Guilds, during which time I visited the full gambit of company workplaces, factory floors and board rooms. I came to realise that you can tell a lot about a company by the degree of polarity between the way the lower ranks were housed and furnished and the luxury afforded the upper ranks. Just as we were leaving the office of one of the great and mighty he asked me my name and a few other questions. "Well, I can tell Doris didn't raise you" he said "you couldn't sound more different - where do you live?" When I told him I lived in Redhill in Surrey he told me he lived in Reigate, the next-door town.

I had time on the journey home to consider this and I realised that a decision I had made a long time back, and then forgotten about, had actually come into play, and that was regarding my accent. The prevailing Surrey accent is as close to received pronunciation as you're likely to get these days. As I mentioned before I didn't talk when I arrived at St Christopher's, though I had no trouble understanding what was being said; so I was taught to speak by very well-spoken nursery nurses. But as I've also mentioned before the Peter's had quite a different accent and, given the time I spent with them, I should have ended up speaking in the same way. It's only natural that a child should have the same accent as their family and friends, how else would we have all the wonderful accents and dialects that flourish in Britain? I assume that at least part of this must be due to genetic tendencies to articulate in different ways - I've always been envious of those who can roll their 'r's' - I find it quite impossible; but the other part is surely due to exposure and imitation. So just as an accent can include us, it can also separate and define us too. We cannot change our skin colour or the colour of our hair or eyes, but we can change the way we sound; at least some of us can. Just as some people are musically or artistically gifted, so others are born with the ability to hear analytically and mimic the way others speak. This is a talent we enjoy in our family and jokes always have to be told in the correct regional accent for effect. I've caught other members of the family doing just what I do when I come across a delightful turn of phrase or a pronounced accent, we sit there rehearsing in our minds what we've just heard knowing that it will come in useful one day. Which reminds me of the conversation between Oscar Wilde and Whistler, the artist; the latter made a funny remark that led Wilde to say, "I wish I had said that." To which Whistler responded with "You will, Oscar, you will."

I don't know if I ever wanted to truly belong to my adopted family, I expect I did in the beginning since I had no real memories of any other family, and what child doesn't want to be part of a unit that is uniquely theirs, and in which they are encouraged and nurtured? But at some stage, quite early on in the relationship, the early bonding that may have begun just failed to thrive and died a sad death. Or, perhaps, it had never really begun in the first place. Whatever happened, as time went on I made more and more effort to disassociate myself from them. I actually wanted people to know that I wasn't their child and as I grew older, and we fell out on just about every issue under the sun - education, race, faith, charity, politics etc, I found that I had a completely different way of looking at the world from them. Since I didn't want people to think that I was racist and bigoted I had to work even harder to make the distinction. I had already decided at the age of nine or ten that I didn't like the way they spoke, it seemed lazy and indistinct compared to the way most of the other adults in my life spoke; so the obvious answer was to imitate those people rather than the ones at home! This I was able to do with ease and developed my diction to such an extent that people often commented on this to my parents.

My delight at such an accolade was usually cut short by swift retribution for getting above myself. From this distance, I can see just how infuriating this must have been for them, and even hurtful, but as usual the punishment was taken to excess and the suffering imposed on me only served to make me want to distance myself from them even further. Habits learned in childhood are hard to lose and I ended up with an accent that would have fitted in well in *The Good Life*. I still remember going bright red when Michael introduced me to his church youth group on one of my first visits to Islington and one of the lads, very good-naturedly, blurted out "ere miss, you ain't alf posh!" I was so embarrassed because I had never intended the way I spoke to indicate class, education, superiority or any other such thing; for me, it was simply about speaking well. Sadly though, we do still sometimes judge people by the way they pronounce words and, in doing so, risk missing what's going on in their heads and hearts.

As soon as I had found my mother I told Michael, who seemed to take it all in his stride as usual, though I'm sure he must have been puzzled as to why I hadn't involved him. Michael's mother, Violet, was definitely not impressed. I had the joy and privilege of knowing my mother-in-law for fifty-one years, and I don't remember us ever having a cross word. But on this one occasion, I do remember being soundly told off; not because I hadn't told Michael but simply because, like many of her generation, she believed that difficult things should be left in the past, and shouldn't be 'raked up'. Of course, she had no idea of how I had been treated over the years, Michael barely knew - it took many years for the full story to come out; but after she had met Muriel I did sense a change in attitude. But then Mum (as I always knew her) didn't take to Doris either, on the few occasions they met. Someone who could give away six children was a complete mystery to her.

It must be hard for those who have grown up in a happy, stable family environment, to understand what it's like not to. Michael is the kindest and most empathetic of people, and yet it took him some time to understand that the longing to know one's origins and to find one's missing parents and siblings, is not simply curiosity; but an insatiable yearning and sense of loss that arises from the core of one's being. It is fundamental to the way in which we see ourselves and the way in which we perceive the world sees us. Having suffered over half my life from a chronic illness (Sjögren's Syndrome) I am quite familiar with physical pain and fatigue, and whilst I would never diminish how debilitating this can be, I have found that I can deal with this if I take it on a daily basis - and it has never stopped me from enjoying life to the full. Whereas the sense of loss that is felt by most people who have been separated from their family leaves them with a chronic heartache that cripples their very psyche, and is almost impossible to heal. Frankly, I'm glad that most people have no concept of this kind of pain - since we were never designed to cope with it. I believe that every one of us was intended to be part of a loving human family and part of God's family - anything less renders us totally vulnerable and incomplete.

Since it was not long before our wedding that I found my mother, it wasn't surprising that she wanted to be invited. I know she was hurt when I said that just wasn't possible, and even though my parents weren't contributing to the event in any way, I didn't feel it right to spring this on them. When I did tell them about Doris they were, not surprisingly, very annoyed and upset. I doubt it ever occurred to them that I might benefit from the experience; it was all very much about how badly I had treated them and how ungrateful I was.

I certainly had benefitted from meeting my mother, and the deep longing was now a thing of the past, but it certainly wasn't an easy relationship to handle. How Michael coped with me in those early days I can't imagine. One day, when our daughter Carolyn was about fourteen, she came home from school looking a bit tired. Over supper, I asked her how she was, holding the back of her hand to her forehead she replied "I'm just a dried-out husk - devoid of all emotion" much to the delight of the rest of us, who couldn't resume eating for a good ten minutes. We weren't surprised to hear that she had picked up the line in drama class earlier in the day, and had been longing for the opportunity to try it out. As with most families, it's those wonderfully silly moments that become cherished memories and that phrase is oft repeated at opportune moments! However, I certainly wasn't devoid of all emotion - I was awash with it.

Having now found my mother I found the elation wore off pretty quickly after a few more meetings. I did discover that we both had a similar sense of humour and were both chain readers, but I quickly realised that we had very little else in common. Doris had a much wilder social life than I had, or wanted, and I could sense that she was rather disappointed with this somewhat overly respectable young person. I had finally found my mother, and pleasing though that was, it was hard to understand why there was no apology or explanation for why I had been given away. I also found her somewhat disappointing if I'm honest. And then, of course, I was ashamed that I felt like that.

One of the good things that my mother told me was that she had heard that Len was making his way back from Australia - she had no idea when he would arrive but he was on his way. I was very much looking forward to meeting him, but we did have other concerns on our mind during that period, and one of them was finding somewhere to live.

At our marriage service, taken of course by Rev Cyril Bridgeland, we were given the verse from Philippians: *Rejoice in the Lord always, again I say rejoice*. This wasn't an option we were instructed; it was a command - and one which we've tried hard to follow over the years. It helps to know that we are to rejoice *in* all circumstances and not *for* all circumstances. Which makes sense since there are some circumstances which it would never be right to be happy about. Our besetting problem over the years has been housing, or rather lack of it. Another verse that came to mean a great deal to us over the years, for that very reason, was the rather obscure instruction from Proverbs 24:27 . . . *first prepare your work in the field and then build your house . . .*

Neither of us can remember who gave us that verse or when it first spoke to us, but it has popped up regularly as we have battled housing problems on a regular basis. We took it to mean that as long as we were in the place where God wanted us to be, doing the work He wanted us to be doing, then the required housing would sort itself out. And indeed this has certainly been the case - God is faithful, but the process of just waiting in faith for things to come about has often been fraught with worry and sleepless nights. But that was due to our lack of faithfulness, not His!

So we were getting married in a months' time and had nowhere to live. Michael had finished college and had a job in the same school in Islington he had attended as a child, and with the same headteacher! Although Islington had not yet become the much sought after London borough that it is now, it was on the way up even then, and accommodation was not cheap. The idea of starting to buy property was risible. Michael's parents lived in rented accommodation and there would certainly not be any assistance from my family, so finding some rooms to rent within travelling distance of Thornhill School was the only solution.

Three weeks to go and still nothing suitable had been found, but then Michael's Vicar told us that he had been talking with the management of the Dove Brothers building company. They were proud of having been responsible for building over 130 London churches, and they now rented out accommodation in the mansion's apartment block they owned. After his chat with them, he was pleased to tell us that a flat had 'suddenly become available'. so with just days to spare Michael collected the key and started moving in a few pieces of furniture that his family had to spare. As there was only an inside toilet, but no bathroom, a tin bath was a very useful addition. It hung on the back of the kitchen door and was filled from the kettle and four saucepans of water on the gas stove. That flat in Cloudesley Mansions was at the top of a long flight of stairs, overlooked a builder's yard and was very small. To me, it was very heaven.

Our honeymoon was spent going out for the day to places like Southend and Epping Forest. I was safe and free and had never been happier in my life. I had absolutely no expectations of a grand lifestyle and was just delighted with things as they came along. But if Michael's job was sorted, mine wasn't, so I started by looking for temporary office work. Office Temp agencies were comparatively new in the late sixties, and I went along to one without much expectation of being offered work - what did I know about working in the London office scene? Much to my surprise, I found that knowing how to work a switchboard, being able to type and having worked for the Inland Revenue, seemed to tick the right boxes. Throughout the five years we lived in London I had a number of temp jobs in a variety of contexts, ranging from a Jewish law firm to working for Auberon Waugh at the Spectator Newspaper.

We married in the school holidays and as soon as they were over Michael would be starting his new career. I decided to launch one of my own. I somehow managed to get taken on for nursing training at the London Hospital in Whitechapel.

I had a very exciting time getting fitted up with the historic uniforms they still wore. A nurse had to be above five foot two inches in those days since patients had to be propped up in bed and moved about manually by a pair of real people, no pressing buttons to raise the backboard in those days! So before I went for uniform fitting I had to go for a health check-up, which included having your height measured. I stood up as tall as I could while the measuring man rested the bar on the top of my head. "Erm" he said "I think you should just go and pop your shoes back on, it's cold in here". This I did and returned to the measuring stick. "Erm - could you just stand up on your tip-toes - just need to see your ankles are working". "Excellent" he then said "I can put you down as five feet two inches, near enough!" Since I struggle to make five foot, I was grateful for his generosity.

A week later I was attending nursing school fully expecting one of my old dreams to be realised. But as Burns so eruditely put it "The best-laid schemes o' Mice an' Men gang aft agley".

In November I got news from my mother that Len had finally arrived in England and was staying with her in Barking. Well, this was exciting, and we made arrangements to go over to meet him as soon as we could. If someone had taken a photo of my face on the outward journey and compared it with another from the return journey, they would have seen a marked difference, the first would have been a picture of hope, and the second a picture of despair. I had been praying for this young man for years, and whilst I didn't necessarily expect to see him with a Bible tucked under his arm, I most certainly was not prepared for what I met that night. Although it took a while to get to that point, since when we arrived he and Jim weren't there - they'd gone to the pub to get tanked up in order to cope with it all. When they finally bowled in about an hour later, they were, not surprisingly, rather the worse for wear. After the first tearful greeting and hugs all round we sat down to talk, except that Len did most of the talking since he was clearly high on drink and what we now politely term recreational drugs. We left as soon as we could and I think I probably cried all the way home. My dream of a happy family reunion was now destroyed beyond repair and I remember berating myself for my foolishness in believing that such a thing would ever be possible for me.

By the following day the pain had turned to anger. And just who was to blame for all this? Well God of course, what was the point of bringing my brother back from the other side of the world if he could barely stand up? I spent the next two weeks trying very hard to give up on God, but yet again the reality of my relationship with Him wouldn't allow that, try as I might. But I spent the next few days rounding on Him at every opportunity, telling Him just how unsatisfactory this all was and asking what I had done to deserve more pain. All rather self-centred since I'm sure that Jim, Len and our mother were all hurting just as much as I was; and poor Michael had to observe it all.

"That's it," I thought, "I'm done with family - it's just Michael and me and his family - that's fine by me".

A few weeks later we arrived home from work to find a letter from my mother on the mat. When I opened it I read "you need to come over and see Len, something strange has happened to him, he's taken up religion to the point of being fanatical!". I just fell on the floor crying. The ever-sensible Michael took the letter from my hands, read it and calmy advised "don't get your hopes up too much - he might have become a Jehovah's Witness!"

So we were back on the underground to Barking anxious to see just what was going on.

What we were about to witness was of a magnitude that I wouldn't have believed if I hadn't seen it with my own eyes. Gone was the dishevelled and shaking young man - replaced with a bright smiling person, who was still marvelling over his physical and spiritual healing. We knew before he told us that he too had met the living God, and that a lot of that life was spilling over into this new creature.

This is Len's own account:

The reunion with my mother I'd so longed for was a disaster. I was a ghost from the past who'd come back to haunt her. She was a deeply hurt and angry woman and in no condition to entertain a young man who she had given away when he was only a child, (not to mention that I was stoned half of the time!) The combination was as harmonious as water and hydrochloric acid.

One night when I was quietly smoking a mixture of opium and hashish, I found an old black Bible in my bedroom cupboard. Someone had told me that you could have a real trip reading the Bible whilst stoned on drugs. Where should I begin reading? The beginning seemed cool so I opened it at

Genesis. I had always believed in God but had never known or experienced Him. A man way back in Australia called Nev Digby had witnessed to me but apart from sowing the seed of God's Word in my heart, I hadn't listened. However now as I read, I was mortified. I came under the sense of a deep conviction of sin and knew I was in serious trouble. When I came to the part in Genesis 27, Where Esau realised he'd lost his birthright because of his Godless appetite, I slid off my bed with his words on my lips, "Bless me, bless me father. Haven't you a blessing for me?"

I cried out to God to do something with my wretched life and forgive me. Instantly I was filled with inexpressible joy and an overwhelming sense of peace that I'd never known before. It was more amazing than any experience with drugs or anything I'd ever had known in my whole life. However, there was no way I could explain it to my mother, or to anyone, what had just happened to me! An Anglican couple, Vic and Thelma Dallymore took me under their wing and showed me from the Bible that every rotten thing I'd ever done, every sin and evil thought, had been laid upon the Son of God, Jesus. When he had died on the cross He'd actually taken my place and died for me. He took my place. Even my heartaches and deep emotional pain and the effects of my rejection and abuse, Jesus had taken on Himself, and carried them for me!

When He died, I had died, and when He had risen, so had I. Now I was a brand new creation. The old things had passed away and everything in my life was brand new!

How can I possibly begin to explain what had truly happened to me? I was saved, born again, healed from my gnawing

*internal pain and delivered from a million fears – I fell into
the arms of Divine Love! Nothing I had even dreamed of had
ever felt this good. Jesus came into my life and I was utterly
changed – ask the people who knew me back then! Now,
some 50 years later I'm still blown away at the grace of God
in my life.*

*I cried almost non-stop for about three months as I wept out
the hurt and rejection that had accumulated in me over the
previous twenty-one years.*

So our poor mother was even more amazed and confused.
Instead of declaring Len a lunatic, we rejoiced at the miracle
we saw before us, she sat silently in a corner watching as Len
poured out his story, and we affirmed what God was clearly
doing in his life. Over the years I've been privileged to see
numbers of people changed in wonderful ways on coming to
faith, but never before or since have I seen someone so visibly
transformed. Usually the changes are gradual, but with Len it
was instantaneous - physically, emotionally and spiritually he
was healed and restored - all the addictions gone in an instant
never to return. And Len, of course, now saw us from a
different perspective. We were no longer that strange couple
who, though related, nevertheless seemed quite odd and
even alien. Now we were sister and brother-in-law who
completely understood where he was coming from. Now it
was more than just DNA, we were siblings and co-heirs in
God's family.

When we set off back to London much later that evening I too
felt like a new creation. My angst with God now turned to
utter gratitude; not only because of the rescue he had just

performed on my drowning brother, but because he had allowed us to see it first-hand. If I had not seen with my own eyes, that wreck of a person, turned into someone so happy and so full of promise for the future that he glowed (I wasn't alone in that observation), I simply could never have believed it. Such healing and transformation was surely reserved for the time when Jesus walked on earth and healed folk with his own hands, wasn't it? Well no, I'm delighted to say it's not reserved at all - it's fully available - right here and right now. If this is not something you've ever experienced then I dare you to ask God for it - I promise you won't be disappointed. It might not be drugs, drink and despair that you need healing from, but there will be problems and suffering in your life that you've probably managed to keep well hidden - whatever it is, just give them and all of yourself over to God. You will never be the same again and you'll undoubtedly find yourself wondering why you didn't do it much sooner!

Just a few weeks later an event occurred that I didn't hear of until many years later after Len had written his story *Coming Home*. Our mother may have found the stoned-out hippy difficult to deal with but she now found the walking-on-cloud-nine new Christian just as hard to cope with. He kept reading her all the great things he was finding in the Bible that someone had given him, that he was now carrying around all the time; which was the very last thing that Doris ever wanted quoted at her. One Sunday lunchtime they ended up having a blazing row all because of a cup Len had left in the sink instead of washing it up. So often it is some silly, unimportant incident, that kicks the door wide open for all that pent-up anger and hurt to come pouring out.

I can only imagine the hurt that both of them must have been feeling. Len went rushing off to find the Anglican minister and his wife, who had already helped him so much, and poured out his heart to them. And then they gave him an instruction, "go home and say you're sorry". "No, no you don't understand" was his response "she started it, she's so cold and hard, God will never get through to her." The instruction was repeated and Len set off home. He recalls that walk as one of the longest and hardest in his life. Why should he have to say sorry, he wasn't the difficult one? And no doubt at the back of his mind was the voice of a six-year-old crying "she's the one who sent me away and caused me all that suffering!" I've heard him say that this was the first time he realised what the words of Jesus "take up your cross and follow me" truly meant, and how great the cost would be. But the Holy Spirit had already taken permanent residence in Len's heart, and by the time he arrived home, he was willing to be obedient.

As he walked in the door to be met by an angry woman, he immediately apologised for what he had said, she promptly burst into tears and fled to her bedroom. This was quite likely the first time in her life that anyone had said sorry to her and truly meant it.

Later, just as he was heading out of the front door Doris appeared asking where he was going, "to church for the evening service" he replied feeling worried since he knew that would really annoy her, and he didn't want the whole argument to start around again. "Wait a minute" she said to Len's amazement "I'll get my coat, I'm coming with you." They spent the twenty-minute walk to church with Doris crying the entire way, and Len not daring to look at her in case she disappeared. No sooner had they got in the door when some kind soul took one look at her and said "I think you need Jesus in your life, don't you?" "Yes" she replied, So on that evening another of God's children entered His Kingdom. Although I never really got on very well with my mother, I was able to see the profound changes in her and see the healing and restoration process taking place over the years.

Len, now freed from all his previous addictions, found himself working in a variety of jobs, including gravedigger. After a surprisingly short time, he found himself called into the ordained ministry and went off to Capel to train at the Elim Bible College. In the first few days after coming to faith he had thrown his guitar, and a few other precious things, into the Thames since he thought all the things from the past needed to be put behind him. In many ways that was probably a sensible thing to do. But God, who knows our beginning and our end, has a way of so often preparing us for our future way back in the past; and he intended to use Len's musical gifts for new purposes.

I had taught myself to play the guitar by the time I met Len but found the classical style much easier to understand than chords; I've also written poetry throughout my life but have never been able to set any of it to music. I may have learned to read music, which Len never did, but my musical talents compared to my brothers' are on the scale of mouse to moose. He has that extraordinary gift of being able to write songs that come straight from the heart - born out of his knowledge of Scripture and his life's experience, he then sets them to music creating original tunes that are annoyingly good. That's not my sibling jealousy speaking, but the fact that if I listen to one of Len's songs I find myself humming it for days - the earworm phenomena. And he didn't just do all that a few times, he went on producing albums for years. In all, he produced nine albums and wrote over seventy original songs, all of which are now free to access on his YouTube channel: youtube.com/@lenmagee4023

Graham Kendrick, when he was doing a tour of Australia, made a point of visiting Len to (as he put it) "sit at his feet". He was regarded as one of the most prolific Christian songwriters of his day, and the only artist I know of who turned down the offer of a gig at Greenbelt three times.

Going Up in the World

Whilst Len went off to college, Michael and I settled into married life and parenthood. The latter was a bit of a surprise to us since I had started to train as a nurse at the Royal London Hospital soon after the wedding and having children was to come later. I learned a lot in my short time there, especially when I spent a few days as a patient on the staff ward when a particularly vicious bout of norovirus was doing the rounds; but what they didn't teach me was that if you are on the pill and haven't managed to keep anything down for some time then it is not going to be very effective! We were overjoyed to find that a baby was on the way, and when Carolyn arrived just after our first wedding anniversary, she became the centre of our existence.

Delighted as we had been with our Islington flatlet, it was far from the ideal place to be raising a child. As I said earlier, accommodation has always been the major problem in our life together, and also (perhaps not surprisingly) the way in which God has most obviously and visibly intervened for us. Michael was employed as a teacher with the Inner London Education Authority, and the fact that newly qualified teachers were leaving London in their droves since they couldn't afford to even rent, let alone purchase local property, had recently come to their attention. In an attempt to keep teachers in the capital they had just set up a scheme that meant that they could effectively jump the waiting list for council housing, and probably have a discounted rent as well. Our names went on the list and we didn't have too long to wait. We knew we probably wouldn't have a lot of choice in the style of accommodation but beggars can't be choosers and we were just delighted with the idea of having a bathroom and not having to pull a pram up four flights of stairs.

We found ourselves moving in the school summer holidays, just a month or so before Carolyn was due. We had been allocated a two-bedroom flat in a high-rise tower block on the edge of the city, just overlooking the non-conformist's graveyard - Bunhill Fields. We were on the eleventh floor of Braithwaite House, the very building where the notorious Kray twins had been arrested for the final time at their mother's flat, just a few weeks before we moved in. We found ourselves chatting with old Mr and Mrs Kray in the lift sometimes, they were quite convinced that their boys were nice lads who had just got in with the wrong company - it would probably have been invidious to point at that they were the wrong company!

At that time most of the occupants of the tower block had been moved there from old tenement blocks that were being demolished. Today you can buy a flat there for a mere half-million, or if you want to be prudent, rent it for just £2000 per month. How we would have laughed at the thought of such prices. We not only had a discounted rent, but because of the low income of teachers at that time we had free milk coupons and various other benefits, which all helped. A couple of years later, when Michael had a pay rise, we went over the threshold by just a pound or two and suddenly all the benefits ceased, and we found ourselves quite a bit worse off than before the pay rise! Later, when I studied 'A' level sociology, I discovered that this is part of Durkheim's theory and a well-known phenomenon!

It was such a joy to be able to have a bath as often as you wanted. It was also rather wonderful to be overlooking what felt like the whole of London. The layout of the building was known as the 'scissor' design since two apartments were slotted together and crossed each other much like the two halves of a pair of scissors. Each floor had a central corridor that ran from the lift shaft to a dead end at the other side of the building. On one side would be all the front doors and opposite a wall of what looked endless cupboards, but which also included the exits from maisonettes on other floors. From our front door you went up a short flight of stairs to the living quarters, kitchen and lounge, which overlooked the city and south London, you then turned back to go up further stairs to the bathroom and WC which were windowless being over the central corridor, up another short flight to the two bedrooms which looked north, from which you could turn again and ascend another set of stairs to the 'secret' exit which came out on the corridor above the one where you started. The alternating apartments did exactly the same thing except you started on one floor and ended the journey on the floor below.

At no time, before or during the time we lived in Braithwaite House, did anyone tell us that, in the event of a fire, the plan was that everyone should exit the building by heading out of their exit (or front door) on the floor below and then find another door to continue down through another flat and so on to the ground floor, without having to access the stairwell and lift shaft. This would only have worked if those exiting knew the rules and left both of their doors fixed open. Since most of the people in the building were working folk they would most likely be at their jobs during the day, this carefully thought-out plan clearly had some massive flaws.

I actually proved that one day. We had been to visit Michael's Uncle Bill, and he had very sweetly given us some money telling us to buy Carolyn a 'nice toy'. We bought her a beautiful ride-on wooden train made by Galt which she loved, but one day when 'tooting' up and down, she fell on it smashing her mouth and lip. She wasn't injured badly enough to need an ambulance but I wanted to get her to the hospital as soon as possible. We didn't have a phone at that time so I snatched up my address book, scooped up the bleeding and screaming child and set off to find help. I knew quite a few of our neighbours had phones and was sure one of them would let me ring the only local friend I had that had access to a car, failing that I would ring for a taxi. There were around a dozen other doors on our corridor and I tried every one of them, banging and shouting loud enough to wake the dead - every single flat was empty. In the end, I had to carry the still screaming and bleeding toddler out of the building and down the road to a public phone box, hoping I had the right coins in my purse. Now you see why I have such a strong relationship with my smartphone.

A few weeks later I was at a 'Mum's Group' meeting and mentioned this incident to the husband of my friend in whose house we were gathered. He just happened to be the Chief Fire Officer for our part of London and one of just three people who knew how to extricate the Crown Jewels from their stronghold. I asked him what would have happened had our building been on fire with the stairwell inaccessible - not an unlikely scenario since children often dropped burning paper into the rubbish chute to set fire to the content of the rubbish skip at the bottom of the chute. This usually filled the lift and stairwell with smoke, which drifted through to the air ducts in all the bathrooms and usually meant a visit from the fire service to extinguish the fire. The smell of smoke and burning rubbish stayed in the air for hours, and served to remind you that you were still closely associated with the food waste you thought you had disposed of days ago! You also learned not to have an argument in or near the bathroom - if you could hear other peoples' domestic tiffs coming through your pipes, then surely they would hear yours! I told the Fire Chief how I had found all the apartments on my floor were empty that morning, and that if I had come out of our fire exit I would have been going up, rather than down the building. I said something like "it's one of those good-on-paper ideas that just doesn't work in real life." He agreed. I then said that I knew we would have been rescued since we had huge windows from which we could have escaped onto one of their ladders. To my amazement he shamefacedly confessed that the furthest reach of those ladders would be to the ninth floor of a building like ours - we were on the eleventh floor.

Those enormous windows were a problem in themselves. The building had an effective central heating system with each room having radiators giving off heat. Unfortunately, the occupants had no control over the actual temperature or even whether the heating should actually be on or for how long. Some bureaucrats in an office had set a seasonal timetable dictating when the heating for hundreds of homes would go on and off and how warm it would be. True we were seldom cold, but the sun shining on huge panes of glass, the width of the flat, would soon heat up the small airspace making it unbearable. There were adjustable blinds inside the double-glazed windows but you know how badly Venetian blinds behave and you only needed them to get stuck at an angle once for them to but stuck at an angle forever, since they were quite inaccessible. So on a warm April day I, and thousands of others, threw open our windows to let the fresh air in and all that heat created by fossil fuels escaped, unused, into the atmosphere. I don't feel the full responsibility of global warming rests with me, but I do admit that I've certainly contributed my bit!

In order to allow us to have some fresh air without opening those huge picture windows, the designers had included a strip of air vents along the top of each window, again like horizontal blinds that could be opened or shut with a little wheel device. Great idea, but yet another one that I'm willing to bet they didn't test in a wind tunnel or anything like the real world. So you have two windows, each half the width of the room, making the metal blades which are opened to let the air through quite long. Being fixed only at each end, and made of a thin metal they were, of course, quite flexible. Three of four of them in each window able to vibrate in much the same way as the reed in a musical instrument such as a clarinet. Do you see where this is going? On a day when it seemed warm because of the sunshine on your window with stuck at an angle blinds, and with central heating you couldn't switch off, you threw the tilting windows open a few inches to get some air, only to find that the actual air temperature was quite low and you were letting in a cold draft forcing you to close the window quickly. "So why not open the air vents?" I hear you cry. Good thinking, and that's just what we did.

At this point can I take you on a flight of fancy? Imagine you are innocently walking along a street in London, minding your own business, just enjoying the sunny, but chilly and windy weather, and suddenly this huge block of flats you are walking past breaks into song. Well, not so much song, more a cross between a thousand bagpipes gone feral and a few hundred wailing banshees, with the drone of entire swarms of bees for some added texture. Well there you have the sound of Braithwaite House on a windy day when everyone had opened their air vents. To stand in the street and hear an entire building vibrating with sound was quite something, it was even more exciting when you were actually inside that building! Though the excitement did tend to wear off after a few minutes. We learned from some of our neighbours that the only way to get rid of that dreadful noise was to stuff the vents with newspapers whilst leaving gaps to allow in some air. But clearly many occupants didn't do that and I think I know why - getting too close to those windows was fraught with danger.

Since the council was not going to pay for window cleaning the windows were designed so that we could clean them ourselves. If you turned the handle at the bottom of a window you could push it outwards until it locked open, leaving a gap of about six inches. To open the window wider you pressed in a button halfway up the side of the window, which was almost beyond my reach, the window could then rotate on its horizontal axis and turn 180 degrees so that the outside of the window was now on the inside. We did hear of one poor woman who was standing on a chair, and having turned the window around, started energetically cleaning the glass. It seems that the locking device that should have engaged to fix the window in its inside-out position failed to do so. As the hapless cleaner leant on the glass the window turned around again with her clinging on to it, now on the outside of the building. Still she clung and somehow it swung back depositing her back inside her flat; apparently, she didn't speak for days. That may have been an urban myth, although I did hear the same story from a number of different sources. What happened to us was only too real and is etched on my mind forever.

Carolyn was about twenty months old and was already climbing over cot rails and stairgates and scaling everything in sight. One day when we were both at home and busy preparing a meal in the kitchen she was sitting at the table with some toys. Before either of us realised, she had climbed up onto the table and made her way across it to the window against which it stood. The window was open with a gap of just a few inches but she decided to get on her hands and knees and push the window open even more. We both turned at the sound, just in time to see her head going out of the window. The safety device had somehow not engaged until the gap was twice the size required for her little body to slip through. I simply could not have reached her in time, but thank God, Michael, moving with the supernatural speed of the terrified parent, seized her and snatched her back in. We weren't rendered silent for days but it was certainly quite a few minutes before either of us could speak.

When I discovered just how ridiculously expensive these once council-owned flats have become I started to look online at photos of the current building. Obviously, the flats are still the same compact size, but it's clear that the windows, and the offending air vents, have all been replaced and the stairwell modified. I'm still not sure how people on the upper floors would escape a fire in the daytime when most flats are empty. I found myself wondering where all the ordinary people who once lived there have gone. I also found myself rather stunned to discover that the owners of Braithwaite House are now in the process of replacing the cladding as it is almost identical to that used on Grenfell Tower.

Just down the road from our block of flats was a new commercial and housing development, that of the Barbican Centre and Estate. This was not designed with hard-up teachers in mind, or the local population that were being moved out of tenement blocks; this was designed for professionals who were tired of the commute and wanted to live in or very near the City of London. Since we needed to find a more local doctor's surgery we signed up with a practice that had just opened on the Barbican estate.

The first time I took Carolyn she was not yet three. We were both quite overawed by the ultra-modern decor. There was a box of toys in the corner but some of them were still in their packaging. I sat in the waiting room quietly reading whilst Carolyn played on the floor. I noted that the other dozen or so occupants of the room were hidden behind their newspapers - no Sun readers here I observed, it was either the Guardian, the Observer, or the Times, with the Financial Times clearly in the lead. Not a sound except the rustle of turning pages. Suddenly this clear little voice piped up "Mummy - where do I come from?" This was not a question I had expected yet, nor was it one I wanted to answer in public; but in those days I firmly believed children's question should be answered as honestly as possible as soon as they were asked. So, taking a deep breath, I quietly explained as much about the birds and bees, and mummies and daddies, as I thought a bright three-year-old might understand. A big sigh from her when it was all over, and then "but I thought you said I came from Islington!" An explosion of laughter made us both jump out of our skins, down came all the papers and we suddenly found that there were real people behind those broadsheets all having thoroughly enjoyed the show we put on for them. The moral of the story: always check what the asker actually wants to know before committing yourself to the answer!

We lived in Braithwaite house for four years, and became part of the church fellowship at St Leonard's, Shoreditch - the one of *Oranges and Lemons* fame. Richard and Anne Thomson had been ministering there a few years before we arrived, and although they were a little older than us we got on famously. Richard had been an officer in the Dragoon Guards before training for the ordained ministry, and Anne a midwife-tutor at St Bartholomew's Hospital; quite a formidable couple. but very much loved and respected by the Hoxton locals. It was under Richard's encouragement and tutelage that Michael began to train as a lay reader.

Every Wednesday a vat of soup was made and a pile of sandwiches prepared for the city office staff coming to the lunchtime service. The service was planned with military precision - quite literally - every hymn and prayer was timed to the second and the battle plan typed out for those taking part. One Good Friday, when Michael was leading the service he found himself struggling not to laugh when he noticed the

Ernest Gibbins clock on the facing balcony, ticking off to the exact second the timing on his order of service.

Before long I found myself working a couple of days a week as Richard's secretary. Their son, David, was almost the same age as Carolyn, and when we produced a baby brother, Simon, for Carolyn, they produced their own Simon just a few months later. Since they had an au pair for their two, it was all very convenient as she could look after my two while I worked. I quickly became part of a small group of mothers with small children who looked after each other, and each other's children as occasion demanded. Since we no longer tend to live near our families I think such networks are a vital lifeline for young parents, and I feel sorry for young women today who often find themselves bringing up children completely on their own.

I vividly remember one Wednesday lunchtime service when I was working in the small kitchen in the corner of the vast St Leonards Church Hall, where some of the regulars were still finishing their sandwiches. When Richard, still in his vestments having taken the service, suddenly burst through the hall door with all the force of a small nuclear explosion, every eye turned towards him and opened even wider when they saw a child clasped rigidly under each arm, both absolutely silent and white with fright. The Revd Richard Thompson flew across the hall with a momentum approaching the speed of light, with his beloved child under one arm and my beloved child under the other. Decelerating as he entered the kitchen he knocked the washer-up away from the sink, and then somehow managed, still holding the silent children, to empty the sink and turn the cold water tap on full. Then to the further amazement of all present, held both children's faces under the stream of water. At this stage, the children felt it was probably the right moment to start complaining about such treatment, unfortunately, the force of the water flowing in and out of their mouths completely drowned their protests. I just stood there dumb with shock, until Anne rushed in and grabbed some towels to start drying them off. Finally, Richard was able to speak and, in a somewhat taut manner, explained that he had spotted the two of them under a large table coved with a tablecloth almost to the ground, where they had been happily unwrapping packs of rat poison and licking them to see which tasted the best. I have to say, that despite any amount of military tattoos, this was by far the best display of military speed and efficiency in action that I have ever seen.

****

It was around that time I made my first foray into a prison.

Back in Redhill, when I was around fifteen or so, I had been involved in some project in the church hall one morning when a message came from the vicarage asking me to go over and help. Somewhat puzzled I went over and was whisked into Mr Bridgeland's study where he quickly explained that they had a hysterical young woman in the kitchen threatening suicide and all sorts of dire things, so could I please go and talk to her since he and his wife weren't getting very far and they thought I might understand her better. This was even more puzzling - what did I know? Notwithstanding I found myself alone with Linda, a young woman about my age who I vaguely recognised. She lived on our local council estate in a very dysfunctional family and had a reputation for being rather outspoken and somewhat disruptive. I don't think she was any more impressed with my being put on the case than I was, and things didn't start well. I saw her as a troublemaker (yes, irony noted) and she saw me as a posh kid who knew nothing about the real world.

After a somewhat hostile start we got down to business and she started to pour out her pain; after a while, she blurted out "but you couldn't possibly know what it's like to be rejected by two sets of parents!" To her amazement, I responded "Yes, actually I know exactly what it's like!" From then on Linda and I met up every so often to talk things through, though it was mostly a case of my just listening and sympathising since I still found it almost impossible to share my pain at that stage. Without the convenience of email and mobile phones, we lost contact when I moved to London.

However, one day I received a letter from Mr Bridgeland saying that Linda had got herself into more and more trouble until she had ended up in prison, and as I lived not too far from HM Holloway perhaps I could visit her. So off to the phone box I went to talk to the prison chaplain. My timing was just perfect it seems, since both he and her doctor were very concerned about Linda's mental health and neither of them could get any sense out of her, and as her family had given up on her they couldn't or wouldn't help, so could I please come and visit her and also talk with them about her background.

Well, that was fine by me, and a meeting was arranged for the next day - but there were a couple of problems to sort out. The first being childcare, which was easily sorted by a kind friend, the second, was being able to afford the bus fare. That isn't quite as pitiful as it sounds, but simply a case of different days different ways and it was a matter of cash flow. We had to budget very carefully and each week a set amount of money was drawn from the bank to cover housekeeping etc. We didn't have a fridge at that stage so I tended to shop most days just buying what was needed for supper. So as the week wore on the amount of cash in my purse was fast dwindling. The meeting was set for Friday and I had just enough for the day's food - or enough for the return bus fare. There didn't seem to be any option other than to pay the fare and trust that we could get by with a tin of beans from the cupboard. I don't remember much about the meeting but Linda did write and thank me when she was back home a few months later, so hopefully, I was able to help in some way; I think I had been her only visitor up to that point.

I collected Carolyn on the way home and wished that I had enough money left to at least buy a loaf of bread, but I didn't, and I'm sure I was berating myself for being a spendthrift and not having any money left over at the end of the week. I had just taken my coat off and settled Carolyn, and was about to see just what could be done with soup and a few Oxo cubes when the doorbell rang. It was Anne, struggling with a large and heavy cardboard box she had somehow brought up from the car. After plonking it down on the kitchen table, she set off back to the car to get a second one, even bigger than the first. She then proceeded to unpack tin after tin and jar after jar of first-class food for me to store in the kitchen cupboard. Now I should mention here that Anne's father was Ernest Shippam, the famous meat paste manufacturer who owned an enormous food production and canning factory in Chichester.

"Daddy sent us another lorry load of tins and jars that have lost their labels" she said "and I was just wondering how to distribute them - when I felt God saying 'take a couple of large boxes to Michael and Lesley' so here they are - I hope you don't mind!"

We certainly didn't mind; we were delighted and quite overwhelmed by such perfect timing. That evening we had a couple of tins of luxury chicken in jelly. Over the next few weeks, we had great fun guessing what was in the tins and concocting some wonderfully mis-mashed menus. Well, once you'd opened a tin of peaches, thinking it might be tomatoes, you just had to eat them!

We lived in Braithwaite House for four years and mostly enjoyed our time there. One of the strangest memories I have is from the afternoon of the 8 March in 1973. I was standing holding Simon, who was about two years old, in my arms and we were calming gazing over the view of London towards the City. Suddenly I saw a great mushroom cloud appear in the sky over the city and what looked like chunks of metal flying upwards. The window was open and a couple of seconds later I heard the sound of the explosion. What I had seen, of course, was the bombing of the Old Bailey carried out by the IRA. Fortunately no one was killed

A few months later we were to leave the dizzy heights of a central tower block and move out to Leytonstone, in the leafy London Borough of Waltham Forest - veritable countryside by comparison.

Out to the Suburbs

In training Michael to be a Lay Reader in the Church of England, Richard Thompson had decided that ordination should be the next step for him; subsequently we found ourselves being shown around a theological college. If this was to come about we would, pretty much, have to provide our own accommodation, with Michael getting just the usual student training allowance. It was even suggested by one, somewhat careless, diocesan officer for ordinands, that I should get a full-time job to support the family. Since we had a four-year-old, a two-year-old, and I was pregnant with our third child, I wasn't overly impressed with that idea!

However, St Mary's Parish Church in Leyton in the London Borough of Waltham Forest, had offered a three-bedroom house to Oakhill College for accommodation for ordinands in training; so in the summer of 1973 we left central London and moved out to a pleasant avenue in suburbia. In the end we never did go to theological college; Michael continued as a Reader and spent most Sundays preaching in local churches, now under the tutelage of Revd Norman Bingham, who became our mentor and dear friend.

One picture-postcard memory I have of that ministry is one Sunday morning when Michael was preaching in a local church and had chosen to speak from the pulpit steps rather than the pulpit. Although we didn't always travel with him we were there on that occasion. Whilst I generally managed to keep the children quiet throughout the service with the usual combination of removal of shoes and general bribery in the form of food, books, toys etc. something went awry that day and I failed to notice two-year-old Simon heading out of the pew. Seeing his Daddy standing on the steps at the front of the church he set off to say hello, on arrival he was swept up into his father's arms in the usual way. For the rest of the sermon, he just sat there, quite serenely, gazing at the congregation; Michael, being the consummate professional that he is, never missed a beat. I was embarrassed by my obvious lack of parental control, but the congregation obviously thought otherwise. Michael was told by a number of folk, after the service, how moving they had found it to be hearing about the great love and patience of our heavenly father, with this wonderful visual aid of a father's love right before them.

It was around that time I remember one Sunday evening when Michael was out preaching in a local church and I was at home having put the children to bed. I settled down to watch *Songs of Praise* on the television. The service was from a black-led church, of the Pentecostal persuasion, of which I had very little experience. As things started to get more 'enthusiastic' I started to get more uncomfortable, even (I'm ashamed to say) embarrassed. 'Really' I found myself exclaiming "this is primetime BBC viewing - calm down!" No sooner had I said this than I found myself flying off the settee and landing face down on the carpet, just as if a massive finger had poked me hard in the back. As I lay there I heard the words "these are *my* children." I had been firmly put in my place; and after that experience went on to learn to enjoy all the different ways and styles in which God's children worship him.

Having realised that we would be staying in Leyton for a while, but not going to college, Michael very quickly landed a new job in a local primary school. A year later Carolyn was ready for school and it made sense for her to head in the same direction. For the next few months they set off each school day on Michael's bicycle, with Carolyn in her little child-carrier seat behind Daddy, copying his hand signals - usually for the opposite direction.

During this time we often had visits from Michael's parents, Nan and Grandad. The children adored them and we always had a lot of fun together. My mother sometimes visited but the children were much less excited, probably because I don't think she ever really came to see 'them' - or me either. I remember opening the door to her one day and taking her through to the breakfast room where I was making bread. She sat down on a chair next to the table and told me all about her recent experiences. Having not long come to faith she was intensely keen, no bad thing in itself, and attended every event, conference and training event that she could to learn more and make up for her lost years, and so she spent the next hour telling me all about it. But it didn't occur to her to ask how I felt about the things she was talking about, or how our church went about things etc. I wasn't too keen on talking anyway since she had barely spoken to her two small grandchildren, who had rushed out to greet her when she arrived, but whom she barely acknowledged. To make matters worse, as we entered the room she had promptly shut the door in their bewildered faces. Thinking back, I guess my feelings would have been along the lines of 'if you reject my children, you reject me - again!'

But I couldn't keep up the sulks for long as the children had found a piece of stiff rope that they had started to push through the large empty keyhole in the door. It was all I could do not to laugh out loud as this wriggly snake was making its way across the floor. During her discourse I had made the bread, proved it and baked it, as well as making some vegetable soup. When we sat down for lunch she took a slice of bread and having tasted it said "this is nice bread, do you buy it locally?"

That afternoon as I was driving her to the station we passed a cricket match in progress, it was a warm day, the sun was shining and I could even hear the thwack of the ball. "Isn't that such a lovely picture?" I mused. "I hate cricket, in fact I hate all sports" snapped my mother. 'Thanks Mum' I found myself thinking 'that's just written off a big part of my life'.

A couple of days later Michael's mother came over for a visit, bringing some of her wonderful home-made Eccles cakes she knew we loved, and some treats for the children. When I had made the tea I went to find her. The children had just taken over a very large cardboard box and, as is the wont of children, were doing all kinds of magical things with it. I found my mother-in-law sitting in the cardboard box, with the children - driving the train!

Sadly, therein lies the difference; my mother had no magic, whilst my mother-in-law made magic.

****

Our new baby was due at the beginning of the next year, an event we were all looking forward to. Having had two difficult births ending in caesarean sections and kidney infections, a close watch was being kept on me, and I ended up in hospital at the beginning of December. I went into premature labour and after another caesarean Peter John was born. He weighed just four pounds. Today he would have likely survived, but in those days it was just too early. Sadly he spent less than two days on earth before leaving for his heavenly home.

He was too ill to be moved from the nursery, and I was too ill to be taken to see him. Had I known that we were going to lose him I would have crawled over broken glass to get to hold him, but I had no idea. Michael only had a fleeting glance of him as he left the theatre in an incubator, all wrapped up in a space blanket, I never actually saw him; things were so different then. When my mind goes back to those heart-breaking days I have one enduring comfort, our dear friend and vicar, Norman, came to the hospital as soon as he heard what was happening. Presumably the medical staff told him that Peter wasn't likely to survive, and so Norman, a father of four, held our tiny baby in his arms, told him he was loved and baptised him; just a while later he left us. Just knowing that for a little while in his short life he was held in loving arms, makes the memories just a little more bearable.

How is it possible to love someone you've never seen so much and mourn them so deeply? Another good friend sent us a message paraphrasing King David's words as he mourned the loss of Bathsheba's baby son. "You waited for him for a few short months on earth, now he waits in heaven to spend eternity with you."

I was in hospital for a while and Peter's funeral service took place during that time, with Norman again being our representative, I didn't even know where Peter was buried. It was almost as if the hospital system couldn't face its failures and everything was rushed along with unseemly haste, or swept under the carpet. I am so glad that bereaved parents get to hold their babies today, in similar circumstance, and proper funeral services are the norm. It was almost as if he hadn't really existed. When I was allowed home from hospital, Michael came with the children to fetch me, and seeing their bewildered little faces broke my heart afresh. They had been told they had a baby brother, and then told he had gone to heaven. Why did Jesus need him more than we did? Years later, when Carolyn was in her thirties, I heard her recount, really for the first time to me, just how heart-breaking it was for her. We talk about children 'taking it in their stride' but I think they are often just as broken by these events as their adults; they have just learned to hide it like the rest of us.

Michael surprised me recently, by mentioning that a few years ago when he was regularly going down on the sleeper train from Fort William, where we now live, to visit his elderly mother still living in Essex, he always looked out of the train window at a certain place on the edge of London, where he could see the place where Peter is buried.

For many years when the time of Peter's 'coming and going' came around, I would go to our filing cabinet and get out his birth certificate and death certificate. They were the only tangible things that I had of him, proof that he was indeed real. Today I would have had his hospital name tag and the little hat or mittens he wore. When we see Jesus, we will also see the nail prints in his hands that he showed Thomas as proof of who he was. I can't explain it, but I do know that we truly need ways to connect with both the happy and sad experiences of our past, and tangible, visible reminders can be very important.

I was in my early thirties when I realised that by not seeing Peter and not attending his funeral, I had somehow never had an official goodbye. Having thought about it and prayed about it for some time, I tentatively asked our friend and minister in Lewes, Revd Peter Markby, if he would read a funeral service for Peter. I don't think he had ever read the funeral service so long after someone's departure, but he could see where I was coming from. So one morning he and I sat in the church and he read a funeral service for Peter John Wells. It's hard to put into words what I felt, but although it was a private service, it was as if having him publicly acknowledged before me meant that I could finally let go. You never let go completely of course, how can you - those hands are still scarred? But the crippling sharpness of the grief was laid to rest, and grief memories became sweeter.

Just a short while ago I was designing a new website for the Paediatric Chaplaincy Network. One morning, I was adding content to the page of resources they offer in terms of prayers, hymns and songs, and liturgy for those who have lost infants. I spent a couple of hours proofreading and sobbing my way through every prayer and song. Feeling broken all over again, and yet so grateful that so much more is available to help grieving parents today.

****

It was a long, slow climb out of our grief. As so many people know these things never really go away, you just learn to live with it and the recurring pain becomes almost an old friend. Coping with other people's grief is something I guess most of us are not very good at. I found it hard when I saw people crossing the road to avoid meeting me - simply I'm sure because they felt for us but didn't know how to express their sadness over our loss. It was also difficult to maintain friendships with others who had recently had a baby, their assumption was that seeing their joy and delight was somehow going to be too much for me to bear. On the contrary, I wanted to share in their joy, and looking at babies has always been a great pleasure for me, and for Michael too. I've lost track of the number of times I've turned round in the supermarket to find him having an animated, but often wordless, conversation with a smiling infant.

****

When we had been living in Braithwaite House I had discovered a sports centre a couple of miles away that had trampoline sessions on weekday evenings. This was great news since I had first been introduced to a trampoline when I was at school. Our gym team had entered a competition and the finals took place in a gym hall that was even larger than our own school gym. To keep us occupied whilst we waited to compete in different events, someone had set up a trampoline in a side room. I had never seen anything like this before and took to it like a duck to water. But I had to wait three of four years before I had another go, and that was when I joined a sports club in Eastbourne. I could never have afforded to pay, but one of the lecturer's at the FE college where I was a student took a shine to me and took me as a 'guest' to a number of trampoline classes, where I quickly set about advancing my skills.

In Leytonstone we found ourselves living directly opposite Leyton County Cricket club, which amongst other things housed a youth centre and a sports centre. The manager of the centre was a member of our church and the family invited us over for tea one day, and before we left he had signed me up as a part-time coaching assistant. It was tremendous fun working with some very lively youngsters from all backgrounds. The coach I was assisting was planning to move on soon and so was keen that I got my training and coaching qualifications as soon as possible so that I could take his place. This was fine by me, and since the youth club paid my fees and travel expenses for the coaching courses and exams, it was hardly onerous.

By now most large schools had a trampoline or two in their gyms, but it took some time for the education authorities to realise that even a trained sports teacher, didn't have a clue about how to teach the skills, and worse still, all the rigorous safety measures that needed to be maintained. After the second fatality in London schools in less than a year, they turned to the British Trampoline Federation to act as regulators. This they did with great efficiency and a set of coaching standards and a three-tier examination system had been set in place. So now, nobody, qualified sports teachers included, was allowed to teach without certification, and then they could only teach at the level they were qualified for. I sailed through the first level, and with some work passed the second level within a few months. So I was now able to work alongside the club coach, and soon took over when he left. I didn't actually need the third level qualification in the context I was working in but my approach was, what if I discovered a budding Olympic champion (not that trampolining was an Olympic sport then)? I shouldn't hold them back because of my lack of training. So I went off for a few weekends leaving Michael running the ship and got my third level experience, training and qualification.

Those who mastered the first level in coaching were expected to be able to perform the skills they were teaching since they were quite simple, at the second level you didn't need to be able to perform all of the skills your students would learn - simply know how to teach them; whereas at the third level you simply would not have been able to perform most of them, this was national and international level championship stuff. Well I could do all the skills at second level as it happened, but I still wanted to experience at least some of the skills at level three. So I found myself helping teach coaching courses with a national grade coach and getting him to put me through my paces.

This wasn't quite as dangerous as it seems, if you can do a single somersault it's not that much harder to do a double, and I managed to perform most of the more complicated moves with the aid of a twisting belt and overhead rig. This is a belt that goes around the learner's waist, that is encompassed in a second, outer belt with ball bearings between the two layers allowing for twisting on the longitudinal axis. Fixed to the side of the belt are two devices that join the outer belt to two ropes. These ropes go up to pulley devices fixed to the ceiling, the two ropes are then passed through another pulley and drop down to floor level where the coach can hold them. The fixings on the belt have swivel clips that allow the gymnast to rotate for forward or backward somersaults.

As the gymnast starts building up to perform the required move the coach controls the ropes, somewhat in the manner of a bell ringer, keeping them taut with no slack that might catch on feet or arms, but not taut enough to impede their movements - quite a skill. When the gymnast goes for the 'trick' the coach has to stand rock steady and decide in less than a split second if the performer is going to complete the skill and land on their feet rather than their neck, if that doesn't seem likely a quick tug on the ropes keeps them suspended in the air and safe from harm. I certainly prevented a fair few disasters over the years, but often at some personal cost in terms of blistered hands and strained arms or back. So with the aid of this wondrous device, and a national grade coach on the end of the rope, I was able to experience a number of quite complex moves without breaking my neck - somewhat like becoming an expert BMX cyclist without ever removing the stabilisers!

I found myself full of sympathy for the gymnast Simone Biles when she bailed out of the 2021 Olympics with the 'twisties'. I had never known a name for this phenomena, but have certainly experienced it myself, and have watched others go through times where what you could do easily the day before yesterday, now seemed impossible. The human machine isn't quite as easy to program as we like to make out.

I eventually went on to take my judging exams and ended up judging at a few national and international competitions, and saw my fair share of people falling out of the sky for no apparent reason.

A few months after I had qualified, and less than six months after our bereavement, Michael and I took the children into the sports hall one Saturday afternoon and let them play on the trampolines for a while. We were just about to pack up when I asked Michael to spot while I did a final run through of a fairly simple routine I had been practicing. I finished the routine with a single somersault and a rock-solid landing and extending my arms up into a triumphant finishing pose. The smug look on my face quickly disappeared when I heard the sound of a gunshot and felt a searing pain explode in my left knee. I fell onto the trampoline bed unable to move, for a few moments I really believed I had been shot, then I realised I had just injured my knee.

Michael rang for an ambulance as I was almost unconscious with the pain. If you ever been on a trampoline you will know how sensitive to movement they are. So when the two ambulance medics tried to climb onto the bed to get me off, I think I probably made rather a lot of fuss. So Michael was tasked with getting my leg into an inflatable splint and moving me to the frame of the trampoline so that the ambulance team could lift me off. I spent the rest of the day in causality, but strangely they were not quite sure what I had done, and sent me home with my leg swathed in what's known as a Robert Jones bandage, it had already swollen to twice its normal size.

Although I was only in my early twenties I had already experienced a fair bit of physical pain, caused by prolonged and failed labour, five abdominal surgeries and a variety of injuries, but I can honestly say I had never experienced pain like that before. Along with my cosy cotton wool lined bandage and a pair of crutches, the casualty staff had prepared me for the worst by supplying me with a small bottle of paracetamol which was to see me through until I returned to the hospital for more investigation on Monday. I hardly slept throughout that time. Michael slept on the floor and I remember lying in bed listening to the church clock striking four times every hour.

You may be old enough to remember the 1991 football cup final in which Paul Gascoigne (Gazza), ruptured his anterior cruciate ligament. Despite having a lot of cutting edge and expensive surgery to repair the damaged ligament, he never completely returned to his pre-accident form. Well my accident took place eighteen years before that event and I hadn't just ruptured the muscle, I had completely snapped it - hence the gunshot sound. One of the two ligaments that cross over through the centre of the knee and which give both stability and flexibility to the joint, had just gone and couldn't be repaired or replaced, leaving me with a very unstable leg for the next twenty-nine years, until the knee joint was finally replaced. At times I had to walk with a walking stick.

On my return to the hospital I was told there wasn't really anything they could do at that point, except put my entire leg in plaster and give me a better pair of crutches. After a month the swelling was gradually going down and so the plaster had to be changed, even so the bruising still extended from the knee to under the foot. The technician changing the plaster somehow forgot to stabilise the unplastered leg whilst he turned around to get the new plaster bandages, and my foot fell off the bed suddenly bending the knee to the usual forty-five degrees - exactly what the plastering was supposed to prevent. He did apologise - when I recovered consciousness! The leg was eventually kept in plaster from hip to ankle for eleven months and I started to doubt if I would ever walk properly again. Actually, I don't think I ever did; I certainly was never able to go out for a run again or play tennis - but I did manage to continue trampolining for a while!

The consultant said that if they tried to sew the two ends back together the knee would be unbendable, and it would be best just to learn to walk and develop stability with the remaining ligament. When half the knee's support mechanism is missing it means that the top half and bottom half of the leg are quite loosely attached. Every time I went to see a consultant over the years they would always do the same trick to impress their students, or anyone nearby who wanted to see something odd. I would have to lay on the bed with my knee bent and my foot flat on the bed. They would then firmly grasp my lower leg and move it repeatedly forwards and backwards, whereupon the shin bone would move away from the knee joint a couple of inches or so in either direction - to the delight of the assembled crowds. I took to walking with a stick for many years, not just because it helped relieve the pain but also because it was quite embarrassing to keep falling over for no apparent reason.

Every couple of years or so I would have the bone chippings removed that had accumulated inside the joint caused by the bone ends repeatedly grating over each other. After twenty or more years of this I was begging for a knee replacement but was refused over and over. The reason being that knee replacements would rarely be done twice in those days since it caused too much damage to the long bones, and prosthesis didn't last as long then as they do now, so you could end up in a wheelchair long before old age. In the end I had to wait nearly thirty years to have a replacement, but they certainly gave me a good one that's still doing well. By that time I had developed a reaction to most anaesthetics, so had it done with just an epidural. I remember it as quite an interesting experience, as I chatted away with the anaesthetist about music to the sound of drilling and sawing and the smell of burning bone!

During that time my leg was encased we had the opportunity to visit our friends the Thompsons. Richard had moved from Shoreditch Parish church to become chaplain to the English nationals living and working in Vevey in Switzerland. We travelled by sleeper train, a lovely journey, and it was the first time I was to discover that the only advantage of being in a state of disablement is that you tend to get waved through long queues - we went through customs in a flash. For all they knew I could have been wearing twenty watches under my plaster, but I don't suppose many watches are smuggled into Switzerland.

Suffice it to say we didn't do any skiing but we did go up on the snow slopes a few times. One slightly poignant memory I have involves visiting a mountain café. We had a very limited budget - the cost of travel was massive by our standards, and we hadn't realised how expensive things were in Switzerland at that time. So one afternoon when we had gone up in a gondola and wandered around in the snow for a while, we were following a path back to the ski lift station when we passed a café built in a cuckoo clock chalet style. We couldn't resist so in we went; the children were delighted and we ordered four hot chocolates. When the drinks arrived at the table the friendly waitress brought a huge plate of home-made looking biscuits. Knowing that the cost of the drinks near enough covered our budget for the day, we tried to say in our very poor school French, 'thanks but no thanks'. Where upon the delightful young lady left, not taking the biscuits with her.

Try explaining to hungry children of three and five that the budget is tight and we can't afford both drinks and biscuits; but despite the disappointment they obediently kept their hands off. Five minutes later the waitress came back with more freshly baked, and still warm goodies, and heaped them on top of the others - giving us a funny look as she departed again. We got an even more funny looks when we went to pay the bill and tried to explain that we hadn't eaten a single biscuit, despite the children devouring them with their eyes for the last half-hour! Later that evening, our friends explained to us that a plate of biscuits is traditionally served with hot drinks, it's part of the price, and had we eaten them all we would have been served more. This is probably what started the rumour in that part of the world that the English are very mean to their children!

During the time we were living in that lovely three-bedroom house in Leytonstone we had a young couple stay with us for a few months whilst they sorted out some permanent accommodation for themselves, they were both medics at a local hospital - let's call them Jane and Andy. Jane was on the nursing staff and Andy was building up a reputation as a surgeon. I used to be quite impressed when Andy would sit at the breakfast table silently studying the medical textbooks he propped up with the marmalade jar. I was slightly alarmed though when he would sometimes rush into the breakfast room much later that day, on returning from work, snatch up the book, rifle through it to look something up - and then sigh with relief and sit down for a cup of tea!

I enjoyed having them live with us, though it did make more work for us. I say 'us' because Michael was always ready to set to and help out whenever he came home from work. From seeing to a crying baby in the night, changing nappies, cooking and shopping, he always did, and always has done, more than his fair share. Jane and Andy were paying rent to the church and I suppose just saw us as housemates. Since I was at home all day with only two small children to look after clearly I could manage the cooking and cleaning, despite still being depressed by and mourning the loss of Peter, and now having my leg completely encased in plaster. They would cheerfully step over the wet floor as I was washing it and wish me a good day as they left.

Many years later, completely out of the blue, we had a letter from them. They had continued to do well and now had children of their own. The gist of the letter was that now they knew what effort it took to run a house, especially with small children around, they realised how they had taken us for granted, and also failed to realise how difficult things must have been for us at that time. I found their heartfelt apology very touching, and today when I find myself dealing with folk who seem to take things for granted, I remind myself that God deals with people's' attitudes in his own time and in his own way, and that I still have a few of my own that need tidying up!

In the way of perfect timing, Norman, our vicar, told Michael about an advert he had seen in the Christian press, he had cut it out, put it in an envelope and given it to Michael saying "I think this is right up your street". The post was for a teacher, combined with the role of lay chaplain for (what was then) *Lingfield Hospital School* in Surrey. By then we were living in a short-let council house, so we knew we were going to have to move soon anyway.

Back to Surrey

Michael thought the job at the Hospital School looked interesting and duly applied for it and was called for interview, I was also invited. So having organised childcare for the day we set of for Lingfield in Surrey, home of the famous racecourse. Having alighted from the train we found ourselves standing on the platform with that slight sense of shock that those living in the metropolis often experience when leaving the city. It was so quiet we could actually hear birdsong!

We spent an hour or so being shown around this large estate complete with hospital block, school buildings and so forth. Accommodation for young and single staff was in various hostel blocks and about a dozen houses and bungalows had been built around a green to provide housing for married staff and families. We met various members of staff over lunch and we also met quite a few of the children in passing.

They ranged from five to nineteen and had a wide range of disorders associated with epilepsy. A few were bright little sparks who had seizures now and then, but most were much more disabled both physically and mentally. We quickly discovered that most of them were quite pleased to see new faces and would quickly come rushing up wanting to hold your hand and dribble over you. Quite a shock for the two of us who had only ever dealt with 'normal' children.

In the afternoon, at the end of his interview, Michael was asked if he would still like to consider the position. His response was something along the lines of "well I don't think

I'll know how to cope with these children and you're not offering the right salary anyway!" To his amazement they upped the salary and offered him the job

We moved down to Lingfield a couple of months later and thus began four very interesting years full of new experiences. Not least of which was Michael becoming a Scout leader with the school troop and my becoming a Venture Guide leader in a nearby town.

For a short while I helped with the school Girl's Brigade which Carolyn also joined. Even before we moved to the school we explained to Carolyn and Simon that the children who lived there were ordinary boys and girls just like them, who just happened to have an illness that sometimes made them lose consciousness and other strange things. We were very pleased and proud at how they seemed to just take this in their stride. Four-year-old Simon, on visiting his Daddy in his classroom, was quite non-plussed when a large student fell to the floor and started jerking around, he just stepped around him and continued the conversation. So it was rather surprising when Carolyn started not wanting to go to things that she had previously enjoyed. When asked why she couldn't or wouldn't say, but I knew it upset her as she had made a lot of friends both with the children and their young carers. Eventually it came spilling out, "because I don't want to catch epilepsy"! I realised that a few weeks earlier both of them had 'caught' a tummy bug at school and had to stay as home for a few days so that other children wouldn't 'catch' it off them. Not unreasonably, she had decided that if illnesses could be caught and passed around, then so could epilepsy! Much as she loved her new friends she didn't want to catch that bug, but she didn't want to hurt anyone's feelings either. Quite a dilemma for a seven-year-old. She was delighted when we explained things to her and rushed off to see her friends again. However, she actually did manage to catch something rather unusual at the Hospital School though!

I noticed that first one then both of the children had a rash of small blisters on their hands, thinking it was from poison ivy or some such thing, I took them off to the doctors. By the time we had our appointment their lips were quite sore. The Doctor took one look and then started to refer to a weighty tome from his bookshelf (Deja vu)! "Yes", he said when he finally looked up "I thought so - they've got hand, foot, and mouth, and so have you by the looks of it!"

Apparently the human form of foot and mouth travels by air in droplets. There had been an outbreak in a hotel about seven miles away and we must have just been standing in the wrong place at the wrong time. We were considered quite contagious and placed under house arrest for ten days and so had to sneak out for walks at night. At least they didn't have to put us down.

I don't remember that particular GP's name, but I do remember being gently teased by him on a regular basis. His daughter was a member of the gym club that met in the sports centre at the same time as I ran my trampoline clubs. So he often stood in the balcony along with other parents watching their children, with me directly beneath them perched up on the narrow edge of a Goliath trampoline and doing my best to catch any stray trampolinists and return them to the safety of the middle of the bed. He once asked me if I got nervous when I was actually on the trampoline with an adult a lot taller than me, and supporting them as they tried a new kind of somersault. All I could say was "not really but I have spent years learning the knack"!

So every time I went to the doctors, and it didn't matter what the symptoms were - sore throat, cough, whatever, he always started with "well if you will practice these high-risk sports, what can you expect?" After sharing this little joke for about three years I managed to wipe the smile off his face - and mine!

One evening I was at the sports centre taking one of my usual classes when someone asked me to support them whilst they learned a new move. I climbed up next to them and was about to start the process when the health and safety voice made itself heard in my head. So I told him to get off while I spent a few minutes warming up; it was a cold night and I hadn't even warmed up from the journey let alone enough to take that responsibility. He duly dismounted and I just started to bounce, no tricks, no showing off, just plain bouncing at a reasonable height. Just seven bounces was all it took. On the sixth bounce I landed off centre, to correct that was something I would not normally have to think about, but somehow I didn't correct it, and on the next landing my heels came down on the plastic clips around the edge of the woven bed to which the powerful metal coiled springs are attached. Had I come down a few inches further in I would have been bounced back into the centre of the bed and would probably have landed in an ungainly heap on my back. A few inches further back and my feet would have gone down between the afore mentioned springs - ungainly and exceedingly

186

uncomfortable, but not actually life threating. But if you have the misfortune to land exactly on the clips (and it would be very difficult to do that intentionally) then you actually get a very powerful reaction which sends you back up very high, very fast, and with the kind of trajectory required to leave the earth's atmosphere. So to the amazement of everybody I shot straight over the head of my 6ft 2in colleague, who made a valiant but vain attempt to arrest my flight, stopped in mid-air, some distance from both the trampoline and the crashmats laid on the floor around it, and dropped headfirst straight to the concrete floor in a manner that both Tom and Jerry would have been really proud of.

My head did hit the ground but fortunately only after my hand had gone to the floor in a last second attempt to turn the move into a handstand, which resulted in the bones in my wrist being shattered. Better to have a cracked cheekbone and badly broken wrist than a shattered head I think. Apparently everyone in the sports hall stopped to watch my attempt at going into orbit without a spacecraft, or even a parachute, and then gasped collectively as I hit the floor. The ambulance taking me to hospital was leaving just as the doctor was arriving to collect his daughter, who excitedly told him that I made such a splat when I landed that I must be dead!

When I went to the surgery a week or so later, the doctor looked at me and winced, and then handed me a prescription for pain killers. He never mentioned high risk sports again.

****

Lingfield was a very sweet little village, and the children's favourite shop was *The Chocolate Soldier*; it was here for the first time that they discovered that ice-creams came in a whole variety of flavours, and that nobody minded how long you spent trying to decide what to spend your pocket money on. Next door was the local garage and petrol station - just the one pump in those day. I once heard Simon having a conversation with his little mate from next door whose mother was giving us a lift.

Simon: Why did your mum just give the garage man money?
Colin: Well, to pay for the petrol of course!
Simon: Well we don't pay for petrol.
Colin: What do you mean - how do you get petrol then?
Simon: We just drive up, the garage man comes out and fills the car up, and then we just drive of!
Colin: So who pays for it?
Simon: God of course!

I wish! We had an account of course, but it just goes to show how children see the world so differently.

Settling Down

The children certainly enjoyed the variety of events that took place in the hospital school, as well as the village school they attended. Since there were quite a few staff children heading into the village each day we organised a driving rota. I remember one morning, when everyone was running late putting one older child in the front and five smaller ones in the back. This was a few years before seatbelts and other sensible restrictions were introduced. Four children went in easily but it was a real struggle getting the last one in - but with one final push I managed it. I leaped in the car and was about to drive off when the children were kind enough to inform me that the door had opened on the other side of the car and the first child in was now on the ground outside the car. It was something I was to learn and pass onto others over the years as we led schools trips and holidays, and eventually our own summer camps; always count them in before you set off and count them out when you get back!

Michael became a Scout leader and was often taking boys away to camps. Always with a huge bottle of trichloral in his shirt pocket to glug down a poor child's throat should he start going into a seizure. Whilst the children and I sometimes went with Michael to Scout camps, I also ran my own Venture Guide company - a group of local girls who enjoyed more sophisticated pleasures such as sailing holidays. One particular activity we both came to enjoy came about by us joining the local Scout's Fellowship - a motley crew of Scout and Guide leaders and folk who supported the movement.

One of the highlights of the year for this crowd was the Christmas Pantomime put on by the entire District Scout Group. In our second year in Lingfield Michael's talents had been spotted when he and his friends did some merry jestering at a Tudor banquet in the summer, and he was duly appointed as the Pantomime Dame in the local district annual production. I would have loved to have taken an active role but was compromised by my arm still being in plaster after my crash landing on the sports hall floor a few weeks before. So I took the role as his dresser, very necessary since every time he came on stage he upgraded the stuffing in his bra and the size of his already oversized dangly earrings. It was a wonder he didn't fall flat on his face in the last scene!

Michael's family made the trip from London to Surrey to witness Michael, yet again, on stage in a flashy costume; previously they had seen him on stage at Sadler's Wells dressed as the Prince Palatine in a silk salmon pink outfit. Since I had just got Michael all kitted up for the first scene I went out and met them and sat with them for the first part of the first act. I'm so glad I did. The Dame's wig was long hair fixed into a bun that fitted close to the face, and when I first saw him try it on I was amazed at how like his older sister, Joy, he looked, it was uncanny. So when he came on stage the first time, looking pretty much the opposite of a drag queen, complete with chunky hiking boots at the bottom of his dress, I turned to watch them all gasp with amazement, then giggle, and then all go silent. Not one of them was going to say "doesn't he look like Joy" with the lady herself sitting in the middle of the row!

The following year however I did get my dream role. Michael was Dame again and I was offered the part of the front half of Jessie, the pantomime cow - I can honestly say I've never had such an offer, before or since. The only difficult aspect was recruiting the back-half. To the rescue came Janet, one of the Ranger Guides in my company. Her only proviso was that she was not going to be credited as 'back-half' in the program, she insisted on being listed as 'Jessie the Cow - Assistant Front Half'; which indeed she was - and a very good team we made.

I found it quite a challenging role, no lines to learn, but lots of cues on other people's lines, and no visible way to express anything, at least not facially. However, I did have some strings to pull. Two to control the eyelids, so a lot of winking and outrageous batting of eyelids, and another string to open and shut the mouth, so at least I could join in the singing. I'm not sure if it was actually in the script or not, but every time the Dame appeared on stage on her own, which was quite often, Jessie would turn up in the background and do the utmost to upstage her; and the more serious the soliloquy the more outlandish were the shenanigans going on behind her. For example, the front half would stand still while a back leg came up and 'scratched' a shoulder, a bit like a dog - we even did the chasing the tail bit; or we would dance in time to the music with both right legs being kicked up at the same time then both left legs. I'd be very surprised if a real cow could achieve that.

But the move we worked most hard on, and saved for Michael's finest moment, was the trick we dubbed 'the slow descent'. Since we were both quite fit and supple we could do the box splits, by that I mean we did the splits flat on the floor, but instead of one leg forward and the other back, each leg went out sideways, making you an upside-down T shape when you reached the ground. So Jessie would stand meekly and quietly behind the Dame all the while slowing allowing all four legs to slide apart until the body rested completely on the floor; even inside our furry custom we could hear the audience enjoying that one. I could also image some of them thinking 'so how are they going to get out of that?" Well that too was highly organised. Just as the Dame was going off in a huff, Janet, whose trunk was also flat on the floor, would quickly tuck her legs underneath herself and pop up, making it look as if the cow's backside had been kicked, and then she would grab hold of the belt I was wearing and hoist me to my feet. The whole thing must have looked like a recovering marionette and we certainly always got a hearty round of applause for that. Indeed one local newspaper journalist talked of "a star cast being upstaged by the cow" and another reporter said "It would be difficult to single out any one performer from this pantomime as all were so well cast and enthusiastic in their efforts to entertain . . . however, special mention must be given to Lesley Wells and Janet Greenhead inside Jessie the Jersey's skin!" Imagine – being upstaged by a cow!

We had four good years at the Hospital School and made friends that we were to keep in touch with for many years to come. So it was quite a wrench when it was time to move on. Again, others pointed out a new role to Michael, and sent snips of the newspaper advert for a Children's Evangelist with Scripture Union. Since we had both grown-up in churches which supported SU we were fairly familiar with this, now, international organisation. According to Wikipedia:

Scripture Union (SU) is an international, interdenominational, evangelical Christian organization. It was founded in 1867, and works in partnership with individuals and churches across the world. The organization's stated aim is to use the Bible to inspire children, young people and adults to know God.

Scripture Union is an autonomous organisation in each country, linked together by Scripture Union International. It is primarily a volunteer organisation with a small number of full-time staff training, encouraging and coordinating ministry workers around the world.

In 1867 Josiah Spiers spoke to 15 children in a drawing room in Islington, London, and began the work of sharing the Christian message with children in a way that related to their real needs. This led to the founding of the Children's Special Service Mission (CSSM) which was later to become "Scripture Union".

In the UK Scripture Union had divided the country up into areas and provided a children's/youth worker for each. They were currently looking for someone to take on the Surrey, Sussex and south coast patch. So this was a large area with thousands of churches all of whom were free to call on the services of said person. Michael certainly felt that this was something he had been preparing for, without actually knowing it, and put in an application.

He was duly called for interview at the SU head office in London, and then I joined him on a second interview where they wanted to check out the spouse. Just to make sure we were really fit for purpose they sent Henry, head of missions, and his wife Margaret, to visit us for a weekend to see Michael in action. This was immediately after the last of that year's three pantomime performances and we were exhausted. As School chaplain Michael would teach throughout the week and then run a range of age-appropriate services in the Chapel for most of Sunday.

That Sunday turned out to be 'one of those days' and anything that could conceivably have gone wrong did - and then some. Even some of the usually docile youngsters had hizzy fits which the accompanying staff found hard to deal with. During the second service of the day while Michael was giving a talk he deftly caught one child who went into a catatonic fit and was about to smash to the ground, and handed her back to her carer, minutes later he was holding onto another child in a different kind of fit until he came to - all without missing a beat. At the end of the service, our eight-year-old Carolyn was helping to put the song books back on the bookcase and started to climb up to the top shelf. Unfortunately the bookcase wasn't fixed and she landed on the floor with all the books and a very heavy piece of wooden furniture flat on top of her. We all thought she must be dead, but once we hefted the bookcase off her we found her slightly bruised and shaken but otherwise quite alright.

Once we had all recovered we made our way over to the staff dining room so that our guests could have Sunday lunch. We had no sooner sat down when Henry announced "Michael, if you can cope with all that, you can cope with anything - you've got the job."

And thus began the next stage of our lives.

Like most of the staff of the Hospital School, we had been expected to live on site in one of the staff houses; we started off in a bungalow and then moved into a house. We had looked at some of the houses for sale in the village with the idea of getting on to the property ladder but, since this was an expensive part of the country, we didn't feel that we had much chance of getting a mortgage on a teacher's salary. When the SU job came up, and Michael accepted it, we had hopes that they might be able to help us with accommodation, as they had with other staff in the past. That hope was soon dashed, as they explained that those days had gone; but they were quite convinced that if God had called us to the role then he would provide us with somewhere to live while we did it. And so were we - ish!

Here was that verse coming back to haunt us:
Proverbs 24:27 . . . *first prepare your work in the field and then build your house* . . .

Well Michael now had a very large field to work in - so what about the house?

The Pinewood Vision

The new post with SU had been advertised in the hopes that the successful applicant would begin at the start of the summer term, ready for all the summer holiday activities. Knowing that it was the sort of role that teachers would go for they had allowed for the half-term's notice usually required by education authorities. So Michael had tendered his notice effective from the end of the Easter school holidays. Since his working contract included the tied housing, that provision would also cease.

Whilst Michael wasn't able to attend church on Sunday very often, as he had his own chaplaincy timetable, the children and I sometimes went to a local church and sometimes travelled over to Reigate where Richard and Anne Thompson (our vicar and friends from Shoreditch) had taken on the parish church. They thought it would be lovely if we could move to Reigate and thought up all sorts of schemes and ideas to allow this to happen - all of which fell through. We had also made a new friend there who was equally keen that we found somewhere to live in the town. Alison had not long returned from living in Jerusalem where she had worked for some years in the mission context. Sadly her sister-in-law had recently died and she had returned to the UK to keep house for her brother and help care for his two small children. We had become good friends in a relatively short time, and like us she started to sense the urgency of time rushing past, with the contract ending shortly and yet no accommodation in sight.

For some weeks Alison regularly drove over from Reigate to pray with us about the situation - yet nothing was appearing on the horizon. By her third visit we were already into the school holidays and somewhat panicking. Just as we were about to start praying Alison blurted out "we can't start until I've told you what I believe God is telling me!" "Go on" we said, eyes wide. In essence she felt that she was to tell us that a house was ready and waiting for us, and that she had been instructed to help with our removal expenses by selling her car. This was both wonderfully reassuring and yet also quite heart breaking since we knew that she had no spare money and that her car was really her only 'luxury' as well as being a necessity in a busy life. But she was adamant that that was the way it was meant to be. I then had to confess that I too had felt God speaking to me over the last few days - or rather, showing me a picture of what was in store. Seeing her confidence and certainty gave me the courage to share my experience. I explained how every time I closed my eyes I saw a picture of a house; the picture was so clear it was like a photograph, and never changed in detail. So Alison, taking a notebook and pencil out of her bag, asked me to describe the house.

This I did, right down to the colour of the walls and window frames, the tree-lined background and country setting, the large pine tree in the garden, the number of windows and doors and their placement and the tiled roof. And that it was one half of a semi-detached house standing, seemingly, in the middle of nowhere. Alison wrote all this down and popped the notebook back in her bag. We then settled down to pray with much lighter hearts.

By the time another two weeks had gone by, our hearts were no longer light, but very heavy. Why had nothing happened yet? We found ourselves asking, why had God called us to do something without making the provision for us to do it? Could it be that we hadn't really been called - that we had just got it all wrong?

To our dismay the new school term had just started and still we had nowhere to move to. On the Monday of the first week of term our neighbours and once colleagues were walking past our window and waving as they went off to work. I imagine that some of them were quite worried for us, and others were probably quite scornful, since we clearly had no-one to blame for the situation we were in but ourselves! What use was our faith now?

We were already making phone calls to the local council to see if they could help us with temporary accommodation. They were neither unkind nor sympathetic, and offered us the vague possibility of a caravan on a local site, but it would be some weeks in the future. We were only too aware that our contract with the school for accommodation ended mid-day on the Friday of that first week of term - and still nothing had happened.

Now I'm quite sure that the school board would not have thrown us out onto the street at lunchtime on Friday - but that wasn't the point. We believed God had called us to follow where he was leading, and that if we were obedient he would provide for all our needs. Yet here we were, with the children back at the village school they thought they had left, just sitting there watching the world go by, with no jobs, nothing to do, except wait and trust. Let me just say, those days were exceedingly hard for both of us.

On the Friday, after the children had gone to school, we just sat in our chairs unmoving and silent; almost catatonic with fear and disappointment. It seemed to us that if God had not honoured his promise by mid-day when the contract ended, then he probably wasn't going to; and the little voice starts nagging at the back of your mind telling you that all that you've believed was foolishness and a waste of time - of course God's not going to help you since he isn't even there; he's just a figment of your imagination!

I cannot say that I'm proud of having reached such a slough of despondency - but that's the fact of the matter and I can't pretend otherwise.

The minute-hand on the clock slowly clicked on to 11.45 when the phone rang making both of us almost jump out of our skins. Michael answered and found himself talking to Roger Pierce from SU - the co-ordinator for the southeast region. "I was visiting speaker at a Brethren church in Tonbridge last night" he said "and though I hadn't planned it, it just slipped out that we had a young family unable to start their new ministry until they had somewhere to live. After the service an elderly lady came to me and said, 'I keep two houses on my estate empty for missionary families returning for furlough - do they want their house furnished or unfurnished? I told her it would almost certainly be the unfurnished one!' "

He gave us her phone number and we called her immediately, and she asked if we would be able to go over to Tidebrook, a hamlet near Wadhurst in East Sussex, that afternoon. We thought we probably could! After that call we had just a couple of minutes to ring the school and ask if they would mind us continuing the housing contract for another week or two since we would be moving soon. They graciously had no objection. Then the clock hand clicked onto 12.00 midday. Our psychological deadline had been met - by a matter of mere minutes!

Alison came zooming over, we snatched the children out of school, and we all headed over to a house named Pinewood on an estate called Badgers Hill, owned by a wonderful lady called Isobel Stordy.

We followed the directions to Isobel's bungalow, basically a manor house on one level complete with guest flat, where we had a cup of tea and started to get to know each other. We then set out to walk to Pinewood from her bungalow. As we reached the fork in the path we could now see what had previously been out of sight. I stopped in my tracks, before me was the actual picture I had been seeing in my mind's eye for the last couple of months. Alison got out her notebook and read out the description she had taken down before we had prayed all those weeks before. Every detail matched – right down to the colour of the paint, the number of windows and the large lone pine tree standing in the garden!

We so often skim over the verse in Joel . . . *your sons and your daughters will prophesy, Your old men will dream dreams, Your young men will see visions*. We see it as something from way back, but it was meant for the times we live in as much as any other. God gave us a dream to hope for, a vision to hang on to, the words of prophecy to commit to in our own lives and to serve as a witness in the lives of those watching. If Alison had not been brave enough to speak out, and I had not followed her example, I'm sure that God would still have acted for us - he is, after all, a loving father who always keeps his promises; but we would not have had the validation that this was indeed from him or the affirmation we needed to start a new ministry.

One thing was for sure, I knew I never wanted to be taken that close to the line again. How little did I know!

The wonderful Alison faithfully sold her car and helped us move to Sussex. Thus began the Pinewood years, four years where the children enjoyed the local schools, ran wild in the countryside, and all the exciting opportunities that being part of the Scripture Union family offered.

Finding a Home in Sussex

We loved our four years at Pinewood and didn't really want to leave; but we knew that we had to move on and stand on our own two feet. We had benefitted from Isobel's kindness but knew we should free up the house for another family. Michael's income was low, but steady and I always worked part-time as a sports coach, so we should have been in a position to start buying our own property. But the problem in wanting to live in the South of England, especially in the patch where Michael was working, was that it had by far the most expensive property prices, with the exception of central London. Having no family legacy or savings it was completely beyond our means. So whilst the 'work in the field' was going well and Michael was rushing round from town to town and church to church, the 'then build your house' bit wasn't going so well.

But as we grew more despondent looking at house prices, God, as usual, had other plans. Michael had been to Southover Parish Church in Lewes, East Sussex, a number of times and had made friends there, and found it a lovely fellowship. One morning, when he was about to begin a week of children's holiday activities, his despondency was artfully picked up by the Rector's wife, Joyce, who persuaded Michael to talk to her husband Peter. On hearing that we felt that we should be starting to buy a house, but finding it quite impossible since we had hardly anything to speak of to put down for a deposit, and wouldn't be considered for a mortgage on our income anyway, he suggested that we move to Lewes. From our perspective that seemed rather ridiculous; if the South of England was the most expensive place to live in the UK, then Lewes was one of the most expensive places to live in within the South. But what was suggested was that we, and two other families who had some money to invest, would buy a three bed-roomed house in the town and we would club together and pay the mortgage between us. We would live in the house, of course, but all parties involved would then have a third of the return on investment if, or when, we decided to move on.

No sooner said than done, and in an amazingly short period of time we moved to Lewes and felt like we had finally found 'home'. We spent eight happy years living with a great group of people and enjoying being in one place for the longest period we had stayed anywhere!

Lewes was (and still is) an interesting place. It has an unusually large number of university lecturers living in a comparatively small town. Brighton, just ten miles down the road, has two quite large universities (Sussex and Brighton) and at that stage most of them preferred to live inland in Lewes rather than by the sea in Brighton. I once heard it described as an 'OK Yah, wholefood and sandals' sort of town. We loved it! Lewes made a good central base for Michael to travel from, and we quickly made friends with more families and folk from Southover, many of whom we still keep in contact with.

Despite only being in my early thirties, I had been noticing a gradual increase in pain and fatigue. By that I mean, the teaching of gymnastics and trampolining always went with the risk of injury, and so I put down the pain in joints, hands and feet, as a natural by-product of my work. However, when we arrived in Lewes I couldn't find any coaching work, and spent a few months just sorting myself and everything else out. But the pain and stiffness, and the tiredness was still there and, if anything getting worse. Realising that I could no longer claim "well I had to put the gym equipment away on my own last night" as an excuse, I finally paid a visit to the doctor who promptly ran a whole battery of tests. Dr Ian and his wife Mary were already friends and ran a home Bible study group we enjoyed attending. So when I saw him coming down the garden path carrying his bag and looking rather glum, I had guessed the news wasn't going to be good even before I opened the door. Sure enough the blood test showed some fairly high factors that would suggest that I had rheumatoid arthritis, and hospital appointments were duly made. The conclusion from those was much the same, and probably would have continued to be the same had it not been for a rather unusual discovery - more on that later.

Knowing that I wouldn't be returning to teaching sport, I started to look at the possibility of continuing my education. Michael had always felt unnecessarily guilting about my not having finished my education, and had always suggested that I should think about getting a degree one day; so knowing that I would need to prepare for such an event I started looking at local courses and signed up for a year's part-time City and Guilds Award in Textiles. And thus found myself, much to my delight, up to my elbows in netting, knotting, knitting, weaving, spinning, dying and sprang! It was a wonderful year, Michael's work was taking him all over the place and we sometimes joined him for weekends and holiday events, and Carolyn and Simon were happily settled in the local high school and making friends. We always seemed to be going somewhere and doing things as a family and we loved each other's company, for that I am so grateful.

We discovered that as a family we somehow had the knack of producing little dramas - much inspired by the inimitable *Riding Lights Theatre Company* whom we had often watched at Spring Harvest and Green Belt. So we made and performed ad-hoc skits, and some much-repeated dramas performed in numerous churches, and throughout the many years of running our own Pinewood summer camps. Even today, when we meet together, there are still certain phrases that produce an almost Pavlovian response in us.

Having enjoyed my textiles so much I decided to apply for an Honours degree in Textiles at Brighton University. I was given a very helpful and thorough interview. They sent me away to get a cup of tea whilst they talked it through and then called me back. They decided that the textiles degree course they offered wasn't right for me since it was fashion based and I was not particularly interested in fashion, but rather in the technology of textiles, they also had picked up my love of history and decided the best course for me would be a degree in History of Design. Since it was now too late for me to apply for that year's intake they suggested I used the next year to do a couple of 'A' levels and they would offer me a place with just C's or Ds. I didn't actually need them as a mature student, but they thought it would help me prepare - again, good thinking.

So September 1984 found Carolyn and Simon in one building, with me studying part-time in the Tertiary College next door doing my fast track 'A' levels. I chose Economic and Social history and also Sociology. Again I had a great time learning with mostly youngsters. I went down well in the Social History class since I could tell the others (including the lecturer) what National Health orange juice was actually like - after all, I had tasted it. I was both surprised and chuffed with myself when I received results of an A and a B. I was starting university that following September. I think I was one of the last set of students to receive a full grant, including both subsistence and fees. Maybe not quite as generous as the grant that Michael had received, but to this day I'm grateful that they paid me rather than me paying them!

****

One interesting coincidence occurred through Michael's work with SU when we met a family in Tonbridge. He had preached quite often at a Brethren Church there, and each time had bought home a nice food parcel - the family ran a chain of local butchers and food shops and were known as 'high-class provisioners', so when Michael and his colleagues visited they never left without some high-class food to take home to the family. He was instructed to bring me and the children along with him next time. This he duly did and we got to know this lovely family. Their children were in their late teens and so were quite happy to be adored by our much younger children. Each time we visited one of them had just come across some toys they no longer wanted and so our two were the beneficiaries. This formed a solid foundation for Simon's extensive Lego collection.

One Sunday, when we were having lunch, Esther, the mother of the family asked me where I came from, and so I mentioned that I had spent some years at St Christopher's children's home just a couple of miles away from where we were sitting. She then proceed to ask me my childhood name; it transpired that she had been a children's nurse at St Christopher's - one of my Angels! Not only that, but she actually remembered both Len and myself. She cried with delight, and I cried because she cared enough to cry! She said how she had prayed for us and other such children over the years, wondering how we had fared. Well now she knew and the family even had some of Len's records.

During that time the children made a lot of local friends and we were very much at home in the Southover church family. Michael and I were both on the Parochial Church Council (PCC) and I was voted to serve on the Deanery Synod - a committee and discussion forum for all the Anglican churches in the local area. The Deanery Synod is the voting college for both the Diocesan Synod and the parliament of the Anglican Church - General Synod. After a couple of years of contributing to Deanery Synod, I was asked by various people if I would consider standing for election to General Synod that was about to prorogue and elect members for a new five-year term of office. The idea of regularly travelling to London and York to spend days debating a wide variety of interesting subjects in an orderly but robust manner had a certain appeal. When my vicar, Peter Markby, overheard one such conversation, he laughingly said "I think you should go for it". He like me, knew I stood next to no chance. The Diocese of Chichester was, despite having the usual broad mix of Anglican styles, one of the most Catholic of dioceses - some said it could even out Catholic the Roman Catholics! I, on the other hand, was decidedly evangelical, both in theology and practice. I was also quite young by comparison to the other candidates, and to make matters worse - I was female! The then Bishop of Chichester, Eric Kemp, was quite adamant, that the leadership and ministry of the church was no place for women; which, of course, made him a strange bedfellow with a number of leading Evangelicals at the time.

Although the ordination of women to the priesthood in the Church of England was still over a decade away, the ground was being prepared. I hadn't given much thought to the notion at that point - in my childhood the idea of a female vicar would have seemed laughable, but the changes in society and different interpretations of scripture meant that this was something that needed serious consideration, especially since I didn't really know where I stood on the issue from either a theological or pragmatic perspective. So although I didn't stand on this issue during the hustings, it was one I was going to become very familiar with.

From a voting perspective, perhaps, it was the aspects that made me such a complete outsider that also served in my interest. Fifteen lay candidates were scrabbling for just eight places, the voting process being the single transferable vote - surely the best and fairest way of conducting any election. Well I did come in last - but last of the elected candidates, I made it by just a handful of votes. All voting was done by post, but took a full day to administer, with the candidates having to stand around all day watching slips of paper being shuffled between shoe boxes. When I got back from Church House in Brighton, in a state of shock, I rang Peter Markby to give him the good news, only he simply couldn't believe it, he even rang me back to check that I hadn't been joking.

Thus began another quite unexpected but incredibly interesting part-time volunteer career with the Church of England. In case you're wondering:

General Synod is the national assembly of the Church of England, commonly referred to as the Church's Parliament. There are currently 483 members of General Synod. Together with the Westminster Parliament, it is the only body in the land which is entitled to make national law for England.

Synod considers and approves legislation affecting the whole of the Church of England, authorises new forms of worship, debates matters of religious and public interest, and approves the annual budget for the work of the Church at national level.

Members of General Synod are arranged into three Houses: the House of Bishops, the House of Clergy (all ordained members, excluding bishops), and the House of Laity, the lay members from every diocese of the Church of England.

I was re-elected five years later coming first in the vote and dropped to fourth place in my third election. In all I spent fifteen years going up to London for two 3–5-day sessions a year, and also up to York for almost a week in the summer when we took over the University. I learned so much during the time and was exposed to so much new thinking and ways of seeing things, I feel very privileged to have had such an opportunity.

I learned to speak without notes and respond on the spot, and even eventually to chair committees. I also developed a certain strength that was required to endure lengthy meetings! This stood me in good stead since General Synod members are ex officio on Diocesan Synod, Deanery Synod and their own PCC, and that's usually just the start

I was also fortunate in that a lot of the time I was doing this I was teaching in tertiary education, and the local education authority kindly allowed me an extra week of paid leave to cover 'public duty or office'.

The average day at synod would start at 9.00 with morning service, then debates until 7.30 with an hour for lunch and an hour and a half for dinner. We could be covering anything from challenging Nestle for their shocking behaviour in developing countries, re-marriage of divorcees in church, to homosexuality and overseas aid.

In my first session, whilst queueing for coffee, I started to make friends with the stenographer. She was one of a team of people who took notes verbatim in parliamentary debates. There they tend to work for less than an hour before being replaced by another team member. In synod this dear lady was present from the beginning to the end of the day, like the rest of us, only working much harder. I asked her once what was the most exciting time of her working year, thinking it would be one of the political party conferences that she attended, so I was quite surprised when she said "oh General Synod, by far!" When I asked her why she said "because people tend only to speak here when they are an expert on the subject in hand, and there are a lot of experts - unlike down the road." She meant Parliament of course; she then went on to say, "neither is everybody out to verbally murder each other here!"

At the beginning of my second five-year term of office, we had elections in Synod to send both lay and clerical members to represent the Church of England at the newly reforming 'ecumenical instruments'. In 1990, Churches Together in England, Cytûn (Churches Together in Wales) and Action for Churches Together in Scotland (ACTS), together with the overarching Council of Churches for Britain and Ireland, were inaugurated.

Somehow I managed to find myself one of just six lay people representing the Church of England at both the CCBI and the CTE, an extraordinary privilege and one which allowed me to meet all kinds of interesting people over a period of seven years. One challenging task I was given was to spend a weekend at St John's College, Oxford, debating with humanists and atheists whether they could actually have a moral compass, and if so where it came from. I came home feeling as if I'd been chased round a lion's den!

The inauguration and reinauguration of the two ecumenical councils started with a complete week of residence at the Swanwick conference centre. Quite a long time for most clergy to be absent from their posts. It felt that the fifty denominations represented - including the Roman Catholic Church for the first time - were all being locked up together in order to actually get to know each other, to take time to sit down and talk things through thoroughly. Invariably we always found that we had far more in common than we imagined. We shared each other's worship sessions, from

Greek Orthodox mass to a black-led Pentecostal singing and dancing session.

My saddest memory was at the end of the week when the daily communion service was led by the Catholics. Throughout the week we had all received communion from each other, with the RC's also receiving from the rest of us. Now we found ourselves sharing the service but not the communion elements. Something the Catholic Church still hasn't moved on. I happened to be in the front row sitting next to the Archbishop of Canterbury and close to one of the visiting Cardinals of the Catholic Church. When Cardinal Basil Hume started to invite only those baptised as Catholics to receive the elements, and the rest of us to receive a blessing, his voice broke. I heard George Carey mutter 'so near yet so far' before the rest of us also broke down. I think everyone in that room wept because, no matter how hard we tried, there were still legalisms that managed to prevent us from having full fellowship.

Later that evening, we had a barn dance for our final entertainment, and I found myself partnering the delightful Cardinal Basil Hume in a lively dance, and who then bought me a beer. So I came away with happy memories as well.

I was privileged to be serving on Synod during the long years of debate on the ordination of women, and took part in the final vote on that historic day of 11 November 1992. That I was part of this is something I am proud of. During the years leading up to that vote we had many visitors to speak on the subject both inside and outside of the chamber. I relished meeting the last surviving suffragist (as opposed to suffragette) who often attended evening meetings to cheer us on, despite being nearly a century old. On a similar, but slightly different vein, I'm pleased to have become friends with Nancy Wilkinson, who represented Cambridge diocese at General Synod. Nancy had been the very first winner of Mastermind in 1972, and was a very useful person to have around if you wanted to check your facts.

I found, a number of debates over the years quite emotionally taxing, the baptism of poorly and dying infants being just such a case. There was one topic which I suspect it quite likely that I would have voted in a different way if it had not been for personal experience. A private member's motion had been tabled by a friend, a lovely Anglo-Indian man who was a brilliant speaker and a very gentle person. The gist of his proposal was that since the number of representatives who were people of colour did not match proportionally the numbers in the pews, we should set up some 'positive discrimination' whilst encouraging them to stand for election.

The problem was that I had only recently encountered prejudice when studying for a master's degree in IT, when some male students had claimed that we female students got places more easily than the men because of positive discrimination. This wasn't true but it really unsettled us since the implication was that we were less worthy of our places than they were - in other words, we had got there easily whilst they had got there the hard way. When words like that are spoken there's no taking them back and there was no way I ever wanted someone to be made to feel second rate simply because of the expediency of positive discrimination. Despite having a good reason for voting the way I did I've never forgotten the look my friend gave me as he saw me go through the Noes door. He had heard me telling of my experience during the debate, but I still felt like Judas when he caught my eye.

****

I spent three great years at Brighton University, and they had been right, History of Design really was my subject. We had some great field trips, our third-year trip being to Poland, and that whilst it was still behind the iron curtain. Lord Taylor, the father of Lou Taylor, the lecturer who had arranged the trip, had been instrumental in the Nuremberg trials and was well thought of in Poland, so we were treated like royalty. I mentioned in passing that I was about to visit Poland in a General Synod committee meeting. A day or so later I received a letter asking me to visit a government department in Whitehall to talk about my 'pending visit behind the iron curtain'. No explanation, merely directions and the name of the person I was meeting. It turned out that since all formal communications between the British government and the Polish government were under strict scrutiny and protocol, it was found very useful to enlist those who had managed to get access and get them to carry 'informal' communications - basically letters of greetings and encouragement.

I was duly given a 'sealed' diplomatic bag, which I was allowed to open, but no one else except someone from the Polish government who would be expecting it. I then received another document to add to the bag, which was a letter from the head of the Catholic Church in the UK to the head of the

Catholic Church in Poland, which I was expected to deliver in person.

When we set off on our travels I had only mentioned what I was carrying to Lou, out of politeness, but didn't feel it necessary to talk about it with my fellow students. However, when we checked in at the airport, it had already been noted on my travel information that I was travelling with diplomatic immunity and subsequently I had to go through a different checkpoint from everyone else. You can imagine the speculation of the rest of party, until Lou put their minds at rest - no, Lesley isn't being arrested as a drug smuggler - she's carrying special papers.

We were supposed to be having dinner on our third night in Warsaw at the British Embassy. But that also happened to be the day that America decided to bomb Tripoli, so not surprisingly the event was cancelled. The next day a government official came to collect the bag, minus the 'inter-church' letter. I was duly collected by car at the end of our first week and taken to a huge church complex where a reception had been laid on in my honour. Don't ask - I don't know either. All I know is the Monsignor was in tears when he read the missive from the Cardinal. I also remember being somewhat startled on entering the room to find myself being greeted by half a dozen priests, in very smart regalia who all clicked their heels as one. It was all I could do to stop myself from responding with a 'Herr Klop' salute from *Allo Allo!*

Of course, most of the people I met with that day spoke excellent English and I learned a lot about the suffering of church people under the communist regime. To say they were being treated badly would be an understatement. I made mental, and then written notes of what I was told, so that I could pass on this information on my return.

We had a really good trip visiting Warsaw, Kraków and a mountain village. We did have one small hitch on our return journey though. During our last week the Chernobyl nuclear power station exploded just over the border from where we were staying. We had to be Geiger counted before we could re-enter the UK, and strangely enough, I was the only one who registered any radiation.

****

Having finished one degree I had gotten the study bug and soon applied for a full time MSc in Information Technology. Thus began my career as a computer nerd. I didn't finish the course but had a great time learning a number of coding languages.

When I applied for this course I wasn't sure if I would get a grant since it was full-time and I had already had one grant. But it turned out to be something that amounted to a government sponsored 'competition'. They wanted only people with an arts degree to apply and were keen to get at least an equal number of women. The reason for the arts background was that they were wanting people who could explain the complexities of the highly jargonised IT industry and convert techspeak to plain English, even perhaps write instruction manuals that people could actually understand! They were offering both tuition and subsistence grants, so naturally there was a lot of competition. The course was sponsored by the Science Education & Research Council and offered just twenty places for the whole of the UK. Places were secured by being one of the top twenty scorers. Since there were over a thousand applicants the first round was to complete a short test at your local college. This I duly did and was somewhat surprised to find myself invited for the two days of tests that were held at Brighton. Again, much to my surprise, I didn't find the testing too arduous and even enjoyed it, but I was still quite amazed to be offered a place.

In the first week of induction we had some personal interviews with our tutors and in one I was told that I was one of the top three scorers, that was very satisfying and I still find it amazing considering how obtuse I can be at times, and the gaps in my early education. It was sensible not to give us our exact scores as we had to work together in teams to produce programs for companies such as American Express.

After I had finished my first degree I had started to teach IT at Lewes Tertiary College which was challenging but fun. I remember when a female colleague and I were working in one of the IT suites during the summer holidays, we were helping to install the new network before the students returned, and she and I were both working at two terminals close to the door. We suddenly heard a group of men coming down the corridor, opening each door and calling "hello, anyone here?" Then one of them opened our door, looked straight at the two of us, raised his eyebrows, and called back to the others "no one here!" before shutting the door behind him. We later discovered that they were engineers from the company we were buying the network software from and had come to supply us with access codes and a few other bits and pieces. Since there were only women in the building we clearly wouldn't know anything, so they went off and came back the following week when there were a few 'someones' available. When my colleague, called Jo, met them again she informed them that not only had she researched and ordered the software but was also mostly responsible for installing it. I think she moved them very quickly forward in their understanding of equality, probably with the toe of her sturdy boots!

I was then promoted to run a 'Job Search Training School' for the college in their Adult Education Centre at Newhaven. This was part of a government initiative of the time to help those wanting to get back into work improve their chances by gaining qualifications and appropriate training. The scheme only lasted a couple of years but again I thoroughly enjoyed it. It was during this period that my centre was visited by a Verifier from City & Guilds with whom I got on very well. On her second visit she revealed that she was actually head of the IT & Business Studies Department and set about recruiting me to work for her. Although I only ever worked for the organisation part-time, probably two or three days a month I ended up staying with them for many years working as a National Verifier.

This was great fun as it meant travelling around and visiting the head offices of companies and organisations such as Marks & Spencer, RADA, the Royal Institute of Architects and major banks and so forth. I found it quite interesting to see how often the reception area would be very plush, as would the offices of the upper echelons, but the further back into the building you went and the lower down the employment ladder you descended, the quicker the amenities provided became anything but plush. One very well-known high street company that wanted its employees to train for the basic vocational qualifications in business studies was so mean with its office equipment provision that it sent staff down the road to the corner shop with a bag of coins to do the daily photocopying. I was quite happy to tell them that the courses weren't on offer to them until they brought their office equipment up to, at least, the standard of the rest of the world. They complied!

I also helped City & Guilds produce some new qualifications in Desktop Publishing - a fairly new skill then, and one that is still undertaught in my opinion. I spent some time on their government sponsored working party on vocational education and qualifications. A very necessary move away from the traditional academic written examination process, to one where the learner was able to prove their ability to perform a given task (enlarge an image using a photocopier for example) by being observed actually doing the job rather than writing an essay about it. Naturally their underpinning knowledge on the subject and ability to transfer the skill needed to be tested at the same time by general spoken questions and answers.

I was so excited by this progress, which brought qualifications and accreditation within reach of people who had great skill sets but had previously been unable to prove it in the conventional way, that I took it to General Synod. By then I had been serving on the Board of Education for some years and was delighted that this was picked up by my colleagues. Towards the end of my Synod career I was asked to lead a working party that was looking at the national *Investors in People* movement and seeing how we might best apply it to those many thousands of volunteers in the Church of England who give so much of their time and expertise for free. The aim being to match them up to appropriate vocational training and qualifications for those who wanted it and reward them for their efforts by improving their CV in the general employment context. After we finished and published the report my last task at my last synod was to present the findings and persuade folk to vote in favour of passing it on to the dioceses - it was passed unanimously and I left feeling that we had done a good job.

It was during this time that Michael and I went out to Australia to see my mother and brothers. On hearing about this impending visit one of the General Synod staff told me that the Anglican Church in Australia was also looking at *Investors in People* and since we would be in Sydney for some of our stay, perhaps he should arrange a meeting so that I could find out how they were approaching the subject. I thought that sounded like a good idea and left him to make arrangements. A few weeks later, just before we left, I was told that a special meeting of their Synod had been arranged on a Saturday so that we could all get to grips with the subject. On the due day we took a train from Mudgeeraba, where Len and his family lived, into the city and duly made our way to Church House. When the Archbishop, who was chairing the meeting introduced me I felt very flattered when he mentioned that early that morning he had collected George Carey, the Archbishop of Canterbury, from the airport and that he had asked him to pass on his regards and hoped to catch up with me soon. But by the end of the next sentence any euphoria soon vanished when I heard him announce that I was an expert in *Investors in People* and was going to tell everyone how it should be organised! The complete opposite of what I was expecting!

Such phrases as "thinking on your feet" and "flying by the seat of your pants" don't do justice to the situation I found myself in. I've never felt so panicked on a public platform in my entire life. Fortunately I had brought a notebook with me to record the pearls of wisdom that I was expecting to be passed my way, which also contained all my notes that I had made during and after our committee meetings back home. As an IT junkie I find it strange to realise that having that book of handwritten notes saved my bacon; I was able to take a deep breath, a quick prayer, and launch into a twenty minute 'prepared' presentation on all we had done. Had it been a later time when I had started doing everything on a laptop I doubt that I would have gotten away with it so easily. Fortunately, they at least, were well prepared on the subject, and I spent the next few hours encouraging them to answer each other's questions.

★★★★★★★★★★★★

Whilst I was busy leading a happy and fulfilled life, I still had the odd struggle now and then in coping with the past. By past I mean anything that happened before I met Michael. We had two lovely friends in Lewes, Prilla and Richard Rowlands, who had returned from the mission field in Africa for Richard to work as a GP in the town. They were very experienced people you could talk to easily and I found myself sharing with them some of my past that only Michael knew about.

Thomas had died some years back and I still visited Muriel, but felt that she neither knew nor cared about how much pain she had caused me; neither was she particularly interested in me as an adult, since every conversation was just about her. I don't think she had a clue about my work or hobbies. To my surprise Richard and Prilla suggested that I should 'divorce' her and permanently let go of a connection that would never do me any good. The phrase used today of such a relationship would be 'toxic'.

I thought about it, prayed about it, and then got on and did just that. I wrote and thanked her for the good she had done me, forgave her all the harm she had caused me, and wished her well for the future. I then made it quite clear that I would not send or receive any further communication. And that was that. It really did help in all sorts of way, and I only wish I had done it sooner. We have met so many wise and helpful people, like Prilla and Richard, who have given just the right advice at just the right time.

****

In 1985 I started to study, part-time, for a master's degree in *Adult & Community Education* at Sussex University. It took me two years and I really enjoyed it - no sooner had I finished than Michael went for his master's in education in the same department.

During my time there I was introduced to the very new Internet and made friends in two faculties outside of my own. At that time computer spell checkers were in their infancy.

Unlike dictionaries which require you to be able to spell the word you can't spell so that you can look it up and find out how to spell it, spell checkers are far less demanding. In the early days they were nothing more than look-up tables that merely tried to match the jumbled letters you presented to something vaguely similar; so you could easily end up with the spell checker signing off a sentence such as "well, there teacher said, it could bee that she has a be in her bonnet" which didn't help folk like me very much. But now I somehow found myself sometimes helping with a research team that were looking at contextual spelling in the framework of Artificial Intelligence. I remember them feeding in the first two test words and getting back a reasonable response, the third offering was *hydraulic ram* the alternative suggested by the program was 'watery sheep' - back to the drawing board! As contextual spell-checking has improved to a very high level so, amazingly, has my own spelling; perhaps by seeing the mistakes I was making in situ I started to learn the correct spelling. Now I would class myself as a reasonably good speller - I certainly know that Mississippi has double everything that's sensible. I realise that it doesn't work for everyone, but I am grateful that it worked for me. I'm not grateful for the grammar checker however, that really annoys me and I always switch it off. I'm not having no machine teaching me how to speak proper!

It was also during this time that that original diagnosis of rheumatoid arthritis that I had been given was being challenged by a new rheumatologist I was seeing. When I mentioned to him that my eyes were often sore, even painful, and that I was giving up trying to wear contact lenses, since every time I looked down they fell out, he ran another battery of tests and decided that it wasn't rheumatoid arthritis, but Sjögren's Syndrome, and not secondary SS that is connected to an inflammatory disease such as rheumatoid arthritis or Lupus, but the more unusual primary Sjögren's that is a stand-alone condition. It's estimated that half a million people in the UK have Sjögren's, which is odd because I know of just one friend of a friend who has it, and I have never actually met a fellow sufferer in person, only online.

I was somewhat surprised to receive a letter on university paper from the head of a research team asking me if I would pop over and see him next time I was on campus. Very mysterious. It turned out that his research project was about trying to find new diagnostic markers for Sjögren's since it is a notoriously difficult condition to diagnose, some people wait for years to have a proper diagnosis. This particular doctor was a friend of the rheumatologist I had been seeing, and when he heard how hard it is to resource blood from known SS sufferers, he thought of me, living locally and also being at the university. So for the next two years I popped by the research lab on a monthly basis to supply fresh blood and have a cup of tea and a chat. I was fully expecting to be included in his Nobel prize when it came, but although I'm sure the work his team did was useful, Sjögren's still remains very hard to diagnose, and woefully under researched.

Two Two-year Short Stays

In 1998 we left Lewes, somewhat sadly. The house was sold and we used our one-third share to start buying a house in Hastings in Sussex.

Looking back I feel the years spent in Hastings seemed quite lonely years and I think we both felt that we never really fitted in. We made some friends and enjoyed fellowship in a local church, but I think the shock of leaving Lewes so quickly and missing our friends of eight years affected us more than we might have expected. The children were flying the nest by this stage and it was very much a time of change. Carolyn married in 1991 and Simon in 1995.

Michael had finally said goodbye to Scripture Union and gone back to his original teaching career. He found a job in a junior school in Maynards Green and realised that he hadn't lost the knack of classroom teaching. I ran an Adult Education Centre in Rye for a while but then decided to try running my own little business in producing heirloom Christening gowns made using a very hi-tech computerised embroidery machine. I went with a friend to see a buyer in Harrods who said he would like to order them on a regular basis, but when I understood the kind of numbers he was talking about, I realised I would need to start a small factory and that somehow took the pleasure out of things. That was another short-term project but it was pleasant while it lasted, but it wasn't to last long as we were about to move on again.

For eight years we had been running summer camps for the children Michael had met in his ministry. We started with just the one week, but soon we were running a month's worth each summer. Each week was for a different age group, one was just five days long so that five-to seven-year-olds could cope with being away from home, for many of them for the first time. The last week of camp was usually for the pre and early teens. On the Wednesday night we had a themed banquet which everybody had spent the day making costumes for. One of my happiest memories of Pinewood Camps is of Chris, who came every year with his wife Beryl as leaders for a couple of weeks, having his photo taken with his tent team before they processed into the Banquet. That year the theme was Camelot and Chris had somehow found himself a wonderful, full-length, fitted princess style dress - and splendid he looked, it complimented his beard wonderfully. Sitting proudly on a stool with his servants around him he was artfully displaying his wonderful Camelot princess style tall pointy hat, complete with waft of fabric on the summit. The problem was, it was a tad windy and the hat wouldn't stay on long enough for the photo to be taken. Cleverly the team had hunted around and found a couple of spare guy ropes and some tent pegs, which they then proceeded to hammer into the ground so that guy ropes could be used on the hat to anchor it firmly to the ground. What a picture! I have some great photo albums of these times but the best are my wonderful memories of great times and great people.

A couple of years later Chris and Beryl were heading up from Bognor to Lewes to a surprise 40th birthday the children and I were organising. Since Michael had been born in January, this meant that they were setting out in the late afternoon in the dark and into a snowstorm. Chris, quite naturally, thought that the appropriate wear for such an important occasion would be his trusty Camelot princess outfit. So rather than spoil the fun and change when they arrived, he donned his sturdy boots and the dress, and they set off on their journey. A few miles in and they are stopped by a traffic control where the police are checking that drivers know what the road conditions are likely to be. Chris winds down his window and smiles at the police officer, "good evening officer" - "good evening sir - going far are we?" "just up to Lewes" says Chris. "Right" says the officer, gazing down at the boots, up to the lovely dress displaying a somewhat hairy chest, on to the beard, and then on to the splendid hat sitting safely on Beryl's lap. "Right sir, madam" says the officer. "Try to keep warm and drive carefully!" and waves then on their way. Don't you just love the British police?

Throughout those years of running summer camps Michael and I had dreamed about having a permanent site. Each year we occupied the field of a friendly local landowner and hired bell tents for the children and a couple of large marquees, one for the kitchen and staff room and one to serve as the dining room and to provide indoor accommodation for games and meetings when it was wet. This meant Michael and a team of local volunteers spent a couple of days putting up the tents, the washrooms and WC's and digging pits for wet waste. At the end of four fun but exhausting weeks everything had to be disassembled and taken back to the hiring centre. Over the years we were bought a variety of tenting and even a marquee by kind supporters, all of which was kept in a shed in our back garden, along with the water urns, huge cooking utensils and a fridge freezer. We had also manged to buy an eight-ring catering oven which ran on huge bottles of gas. The kind friends who lent us their field also supplied us with electricity which meant we could run projectors, music players, lighting at night and keep food and milk fresh in the fridge freezer.

Margaret, one of our dear friends who helped me on the catering team every year, had a father who ran a local butcher's shop. So his van would arrive on the field most days to deliver our meat order. Gandalf, our wonderful pooch, a cross between a husky and a golden retriever, also regarded camp month as the best time of the year, as he could run free all day and be adored by all the children. Naturally he made firm friends with Mr Newman, the butcher, and ran to help open the gate as soon as he saw the van arriving. Mr Newman's first task was to supply him with the bone of the day, especially selected for such an important dog. That sorted Gandalf went off for some down time, while we helped unpack the meat delivery.

One day, however, something was going on and Gandalf's bone wasn't forthcoming immediately since Mr Newman was off over the other side of the field looking at something interesting. Gandalf, not being a patient sort of creature decided that, since the back door of the van was already open, it would be sensible for him to help himself. He didn't manage to find his bone, but he made up for it - as we headed back to the van we saw him darting into the bushes wearing a necklace made of three of four strings of sausages. He did have the grace to look slightly sheepish when he returned sometime later to his self-appointed guard duty.

We soon discovered that using first class food supplies meant there was much less wastage, both in terms of the cooking process and the amount of uneaten food. In the end it was only a little more expensive than the catering supplies we had tried previously, and most certainly better value for money as well as much tastier. We produced everything in our marquee kitchen from lasagna, Sunday roasts, to scones, sponge cakes, and tons of flapjacks! We collected our milk daily from the local farm, straight from the cooling machine and brought it back in a vast plastic container. This was kept in a fridge with most of the shelves removed and allowed to settle until the cream, of which there was lots, had risen to the top. We then syphoned it off and used it for serving with the breakfast porridge, or depending on the day, Bircher muesli. The latter was a Swiss oatmeal dish that I had discovered in the *Women's Own* cookery book that Carolyn bought me for my birthday a few months before she was born (she was always a tad precocious)! It consisted of a huge billy can being half-filled with the cream into which was poured vast amounts of oats, dried fruit and honey or brown sugar. It was then left to soak overnight while it turned into a delicious creamy mix. In the morning some chopped nuts and apples were added and some sliced bananas. The resulting dish was an all-time favourite, I don't remember any of it ever being wasted.

However, we longed to have a permanent site that could be used throughout the year and which wouldn't need assembling and disassembling each time. We also dreamed that we could use such a place as a training centre where we could train others in the skills of running camps and holidays. I even had plans of using City & Guilds to help produce a vocational qualification in "Summer Camp Leadership". Sadly this dream was never realised, and we certainly found it hard not to be jealous when Michael's colleague, who did the same job with SU in Kent, was given a permanent site by some wonderfully kind benefactors. Di and Maureen Lewis certainly made good use of Long Barn which is still being run by the next generation.

I like to think those hundreds of children and young people who attended or served at our Pinewood Camps over the years have some happy memories stored away. Indeed, we have been told a few times by those who were children then "camp was my highlight of the year". It certainly was one of my highlights and even after all these years it holds a special place in our family memories.

But now we took down the tents and marquees for a last time and passed then on to others who were setting up their own summer camps. The reason that I didn't stand for election for a fourth term of office on Synod was that we were moving on again and leaving Lewes and the Diocese of Chichester.

When we saw the advert for the role of Manager of Carroty Wood, a Christian holiday centre for children and young people based in Tonbridge in Kent, this seemed like a golden opportunity. It was a strange time, because Michael had long considered working as a Diocesan Youth & Children's Advisor for the Church of England. He had applied to Exeter Diocese for just such a post, had been interviewed and was waiting to hear the results when we were summonsed for an interview at Carroty Wood, just before the interview he heard that he had been offered the job. Having said 'probably, yes' to Exeter, we were somewhat confused when he was also offered the Tonbridge job. Since the centre management post, with both of us involved, seemed like the answer to our dreams, that was the one we went for. We spent two years there, and had some fun and learned a lot, but our 'dream' wasn't realised. All the things we had wanted to do, and which at the time seemed why the trustees had appointed us, were met with a resistance that was hard to overcome. Such an impasse was reached that we left and Michael returned to teaching.

The only problem was, as usual, accommodation. We had let go of the house we had started to buy in Hastings when we moved into Carroty Wood. So here we were, for a second time, wondering where we were going to live and how we were going to live. You would think that having experienced this before it would be easier to trust the second time round. Well, although we did have that memory of the incredible eleventh-hour rescue in our mental scrapbook - it still left us reeling. We ended up moving to Hereford and starting over there.

The Hereford Years

When Michael was a teenager he had a number of friends from the church youth group. One went by the name of Peter Strevens, the two of them were to form a lifelong friendship, sharing and swapping the roles of best man at our weddings and God parent to our respective children.

Peter was an accountant and he and Janet moved to Hereford after they married, which was not long before we got married. A few times every year we would make our way over to Hereford, from wherever we might be living at the time, to reconnect. Over the years we had grown to know Hereford well, and were greeted by name whenever we went to St Peter's church with them.

So when, yet again we found ourselves with no jobs and nowhere to live, Hereford seemed like a good place to start over. I was developing my website building skills and quickly got a temporary job as an IT help consultant. Michael, meanwhile, was able to sign on to agencies looking for temporary teachers.

We rented a lovely little place called 'Willow Cottage', from there we moved to a town house that Peter and Janet purchased to help us out as we struggled for a while, and then we rented a lovely old cottage called 'The Mill' since it had once been a water mill.

We hadn't been in Hereford long when a post came up for a research assistant at The Royal National College for the Blind, which I applied for and was delighted to get. Founded in

London in 1872, after a number of moves the RNC opened its residential college in Hereford in 1978. My role was with the research and development team that was working on making the Internet more accessible to blind and partially sighted students - my particular task was developing online learning courses - that were becoming all the rage in the sighted world - but with absolutely no visuals at all. Think of a Zoom meeting underway with no one able to see that someone else has joined them - so we had to make up audio clues like a knock on the door, the squeak of the door opening, then footsteps and the drawing up of a chair.

I hadn't long been working on that project when I was sent off to London to a conference on using technology in education for the blind and partially sighted. It was there that I met Steven Landau - a great guy from New York who had invented the *Talking Tactile Tablet* and was hoping to find some interest in his work in the UK. I loved his device at first sight and persuaded him to come and spend a few days at RNC to talk through the possibilities.

The Talking Tactile Tablet, or T3 as I rebranded it, become my next project and I was to work with the American team to develop it over the next couple of years. According to Wikipedia the T3 is:

. . . a graphic tablet with a touch surface that can be used as an input device that uses swell paper to create 3D overlays and connects audio files to parts of the overlays. The device is connected to a computer and run with a programme CD, and has a tactile surface which produces touchable icons that provide audio feedback when they are pressed. It can be used to help

visually impaired users to interpret diagrams, charts and maps by producing a tactile, touchable image, and audio feedback.

Quite quickly I found myself travelling all over the UK and Europe taking the T3 to a variety of schools, colleges and other institutions. Michael often did duty as my driver and assistant presenter since to do all that on my own was sometimes too demanding. This was noticed by the RNC management who then appointed him as a research assistant in the T3 department I was now running. His teaching background made him very useful in producing educational content for the programs which I and others on the team were now developing. So for a few years we travelled hither and thither and had some great adventures. Not least was getting lost in Brussels on the way to an appointment (just a bit before Satnav was released). We stopped, I flagged down a taxi, told the drive to go to the given address, actually said the words to Michael "follow that taxi"! We got there just in the nick of time.

We took the T3 to the Education Department at the Anglia Ruskin University in Chelmsford, where its potential to help sighted learners, particularly those with learning difficulties, was immediately spotted. It was also the start of the idea that the technology could also help with children's learning generally since it involved the use of more than one of the senses.

We were invited to join an inter-university project that was just starting research into developing a machine that could 'print' raised material on a variety of substrates. So we actually found ourselves involved in the early development of

3D printing! Since I had a master's degree I was invited to join with five others who were hoping to get their PhD's through the project. It was yet another degree where everything was paid for! I was appointed a tutor, Dr Theodora Papadopoulos, a lovely Greek lady who we got to know over the next couple of years. Michael, Theodora and I were sent off to present papers at a conference in Munich in the middle of winter. I have memories of us trudging through the snow to get to the venue. In the evening we went to a reception at the Rathaus (Town Hall), where I remember picking my way through a great buffet spread before us. Seeing a large plate of cream cheese, I took a nice little slice and some savoury biscuits to spread it on, that and some salad and I was a happy bunny. That is until I took my first mouthful of the cream cheese, I choked and only just managed to swallow rather than spit it out. Seeing my distress, an English-speaking member of staff came rushing up to see if I was alright. 'Oh my goodness, it tasted just like what we would call lard' I told him. 'That's because it is what you would call lard' he replied! Apparently Schweineschmalz is considered a delicacy in that part of Germany.

I fared better when I went with Steven Landau to present papers at a conference in Dublin University. To our surprise one of the conference venues was the Guinness Brewery and we got to spend two days presenting there and sampling the wares. It is true, Guinness does taste better in Ireland, and even better in Dublin!

Since I had started at RNC, the Principal who had worked so hard to raise the profile of the college, had retired. So a new principal was appointed along with a business manager.

Naturally Steven, as the intellectual owner of the T3 had legally safeguarded his property whilst giving my team free reign to develop the operating system and produce educational content. This was a system that worked well, that is until the new business manager came on the scene. Unbeknown to any of the rest of us, T3 machines were sent to a UK university research department (who knew nothing of the legal restraints on the product) where they were asked to back engineer the device and produce a new 'similar' product for the commercial market. When I discovered this I had no choice but to present the evidence to the Principal, who seemed not to be as concerned as I thought she should be. Very shortly after this it was decided to 'reshape' the research team. Along with a number of members of staff, including some very long-term teaching staff, Michael, myself, and the rest of the T3 team found that our jobs were being terminated and that we had to 'reapply' for them.

It wasn't too surprising to find that our new roles would be solely under the management of the business manager, who had no academic or research background whatsoever! To the surprise of many of our colleagues, though not to some who were aware of what was going on, we said 'no thank you' and walked away.

It was also not surprising when less than a year later we heard that both the Principal and the business manager had 'resigned'. It still saddens me today that all that work and development was largely lost (and I didn't get to finish my PhD) simply due to the dishonesty of a colleague. On a number of occasions we had seen both visually impaired teachers and students weep when they experienced the T3 for the first time. "Finally, I can understand the map of the world" one of them had said.

One strange thing that happened whilst were part of the Chelmsford inter-university research team, just as the project was winding up, was to do with one of my fellow PhD students.

Just as we were leaving RNC news broke of a terrorist attack at Glasgow airport. I was shocked to receive a phone call the following day from the professor who had lead the project, saying that, along with all the other members of the team, we would be asked to do a phone interview with the police since one of our colleagues, Kafeel Ahmed, was one of the bombers. We remembered Kafeel coming directly from Pakistan, starting a couple of weeks later than the rest of us, but quickly catching up and fitting in. He was very quiet and polite and on the few occasions I spent any time with him, I found him very pleasant to talk with. It seems that he went off with his cousin at the end of term, and the project, and came back having been 'turned'. Throughout the project Kafeel had been working on the setting of the liquid plastic on to various substrates to form the tactile images we were working on. His doctorate has been all about fluid dynamics; so it was all the more amazing to find that he had made so many basic mistakes when he turned terrorist!

Wikipedia:
The Glasgow Airport attack was a terrorist ramming attack which occurred on 30 June 2007, at 15:11 BST, when a dark green Jeep Cherokee loaded with propane canisters was driven at the glass doors of the Glasgow Airport terminal and set

ablaze. The car's driver was severely burnt in the ensuing fire, and five members of the public were injured, none seriously. Some injuries were sustained by those assisting the police in detaining the occupants. A close link was quickly established to the 2007 London car bombs the previous day.

Both of the car's occupants were apprehended at the scene. Within three days, Scotland Yard had confirmed that eight people had been taken into custody in connection with this incident and that in London.

Police identified the two men as Bilal Abdullah, a British-born, Muslim doctor of Iraqi descent working at the Royal Alexandra Hospital, and Kafeel Ahmed, also known as Khalid Ahmed, an Indian-born engineer and the driver, who was treated for fatal burns at the same hospital.

The newspaper *The Australian* alleged that a suicide note indicated that the two had intended to die in the attack. Kafeel Ahmed died from his injuries on 2 August. Bilal Abdullah was later found guilty of conspiracy to commit murder and was sentenced to life imprisonment with a minimum of 32 years.

We certainly were interviewed by the police, but just like all the others in the team, we hadn't a clue of what was going on in Kafeel's mind. We were just off to America for the first of our visits to Yellowstone, and having been to the USA a few times before, knew that you usually have to answer a battery of questions before being granted entry, and I seem to recall that one of them was something like "have you recently associated with anyone involved with terrorist activity?" To that end we did have a letter from the university explaining that we were merely colleagues, but fortunately the hardest questions we had to answer on that trip were "are you carrying any plant species?" and "do you intend to commit any moral turpitude?" The answer to that last question that I've always wanted to write, instead of just plain "No" is - "If I was planning to commit moral turpitude do you really thing I would tell you about it?"

So it was a serious blow for us to have to leave a job that we both very much enjoyed, and all because of the reprehensible behaviour of others. But, as always, the next thing was waiting for us, and while we were making our final decision on the college situation I put in an application to Hereford Council who were looking for a manager for their regional museums. Ever since I had studied History of Design I had fancied working in a museum, and now I found myself with five to look after.

When we first moved to Hereford, the cottage we lived in was in a village Creden Hill, a couple of miles outside Hereford City. We didn't know it, but it happens to be the base of the SAS regiments. We soon got used to the background sound of them practising on the firing ranges just over the road from us. Michael's godson, Richard, son of our friends the Strevens, had joined the army some years before and sometimes came back home to Hereford for R&R and training. Over a meal with the family I mentioned that I had recently discovered some of my family history, and met an uncle who had told me all about the Great Uncle Paddy. Naturally this impressed Richard and he mentioned it in passing to a mate of his who was Chaplain to the SAS. He too was surprised and wanted to meet a relative of the SAS legend. I then received an invitation to the base to meet some of the officers, and to see Paddy's statue that stands in the grounds - identical to the one in the town square of his hometown Newtownards in Northern Ireland.

Then I received an invitation to a celebratory dinner in the officer's mess. Simon accompanied me on this occasion and it certainly felt odd being asked by these (mostly incredibly tall) elite officers if they could 'shake me by the hand', just so that they could say they had met a relative of Colonel Paddy! We were duly shown, with great solemnity, the display cabinets in pride of place containing Paddy's handgun, one of his helmets and a few other personal effects. We were also told that there is a small museum in France dedicated to Paddy and his work behind enemy lines in the latter part of the war, apparently it features one of his tin helmets with a dent in the side where a bullet had bounced off.

At one stage during the evening we were standing around having drinks when the room suddenly went quiet. It was a warm summer evening and I was standing just outside the open French windows, cricking my neck as I talked to one of the senior officers, when I saw his gaze go over my head and upwards, I turned and duly followed his gaze and then stopped in my tracks when I saw a pair of feet in combat boots dangling in the air in front of me. I continued upwards until I saw the smiling face of a soldier who had magically made his parachute stop its descent just before he reached the ground, causing him to hover in midair. He then pulled a string, finished the descent and 'stepped' down onto the ground saluting as he did so. When the laughter due to my incredulous face was over it was duly explained that some of 'the boys' had been out on a training trip and were just coming back for supper!

We were to visit the base a few times, on one occasion taking some of the family to be photographed around Paddy's statue. One visit that stays vividly in my memory was on Remembrance Sunday, when Michael and I were invited to join the service that takes place on the parade grounds in the base. Almost all of the other civilians there were parents and family of serving SAS soldiers, or indeed relatives of those who had recently died in service. So it was an enormous privilege to be there.

This was at a time when a lot of the regiment were in Afghanistan, and those who had just returned, or were waiting to go, filled the parade ground. They were joined by about twenty or so soldiers in either civies or battle dress who had only just returned to the UK that morning. At eleven o'clock we stood on a platform overlooking the parade ground and all the young men and women standing silently, with their hands behind their backs and their heads bowed. After a minute or so we could hear the buzz of a helicopter in the distance coming towards us. I remember thinking 'this is odd, you would have thought that all local aircraft would have been grounded for this one hour of the year'. But as we watched it approach it slowed as it followed a path right over the parade ground; as it passed over we could see the back was open with people standing in the doorway, just as they started to disappear the Last Post sounded, and thousands of poppies fell from the back of the helicopter. In true SAS style the windspeed and everything had been perfectly accounted for and the poppies floated down landing on and around the ranks of young people, and those parents mourning their losses. I still tear up when I remember those precious few moments and how honoured we were to share something that is generally hidden from the public gaze.

Before I left the museum service I started to work with the regiment and some of the staff of the SAS London HQ on a project to hold an SAS exhibition, using some of the wartime jeeps they made famous, perhaps reconstructing a scene from one of the many paintings made on the subject. Sadly that wasn't to be because just as the project started I felt led to start another job. I hope we would have made a better job of it than *SAS: Rogue Heroes* - a British television historical drama series shown in 2023, depicting the origins of the British Army Special Air Service. It is sad when the stories of real lives and events are spoiled by over dramatisation. The Belfast Telegraph published a complaint by Fiona Ferguson, my second cousin and niece of Col Paddy, who said "there was more to him than "a drunk Irishman".

Fiona has shared her recollections of her uncle in a new book called *SAS Brothers in Arms* by historian Damien Lewis.

Mr Lewis conducted interviews with Mayne's family, something they claim the creator and writers of *SAS Rogue Heroes* did not. He also read letters written by Mayne belonging to Fiona and the family. "The more I went through these documents I discovered Mayne's humanity," said Mr Lewis. "It shone through." "You wouldn't make someone who is a drunken thug your discipline officer. It's nonsense to portray him as a thug and a drunken lout - there is no evidence of that. This was someone who, on return to civilian life, was made Secretary to the Law Society of Northern Ireland."

I spent just a few years managing museums in Hereford, Ledbury, and Leominster, with Michael joining the team of volunteers that ran the Ledbury Museum.

My office was based in the Hereford Museum and Art Gallery, and I could see the Cathedral out of my window. Most Wednesdays would see me popping across the road to attend the lunchtime service there - I still love a good cathedral service!

One memory of the museum takes me back to a day when a colleague and I were checking the condition of the art collection that was not currently on show in the gallery, and which consisted of a few hundred paintings. At that time it was stored on the top floor of the museum building. It was shortly to be moved to the new purpose built, multi-million-pound Museum Resource and Learning Centre just a few streets away and we were preparing for the move. Given that we were on the fourth floor of a tall building we were both somewhat surprised to suddenly hear the window behind us being forced open. We turned, and to our amazement a firefighter - complete with helmet - was stepping into the room. My colleague was young and single, but I too was standing with my mouth open hearing *I'm holding out for a hero* playing in the background of this scene straight out of a Hollywood movie. We closed our mouths when we realised that two more officers were joining him.

Apparently the local fire station had just taken delivery of a replacement cherry picker and the officer wanted to check that it could reach our top floor, whilst doing so he also noticed that we had no lock on the windows. It seemed that our collection was top of the list of 'save and rescue' objects and artifacts in the city. When all three of them had joined us the senior officer, knowing that we had three early Turner's asked if he could see them. "This is a treat" he said to the two youngsters "these are the genuine article!" "Do you think I could actually hold one" he asked, so sweetly that I couldn't possibly refuse him. So I duly reached one down from the shelf, much to his delight, and gave it to him - he practically hugged it! Eventually he handed it to one of the other officers, who took it, gazed at it, and just kept saying Wow! Wow! Finally he put it into the hands of the third officer, who looked at it, shrugged her shoulders and said "so who's Turner - is he a local?" Witness four people totally at a loss for words.

****

So having found a lovely place to live and a good job, why did we move yet again? Looking back it's quite hard to answer. Yet another advert was pointed out to us, this time for an 'Operations Manager' for two town centre churches in Cheltenham. Managing the staff and volunteers of a large congregation certainly appealed. Michael's reaction a few years back on the employment situation was "well you've followed me around for years and gone wherever I've led, now it's your turn." Not only did Michael strongly encourage me to apply for my first degree, and supported me all the way from then on; but he also made it clear that he wanted me to gain qualifications so that if I ever wanted to leave I would be able to support myself. I still think of that as one of the most unselfish and loving statements I've ever heard!

Just recently our entire family had a two-week family holiday sharing a house in Cumbria. The children and grandchildren were all there, ranging from seven to twenty-eight. Holly, second eldest grandchild asked at the supper table one evening "Nana, did you really get married when you were only eighteen?" "Yes - and I'm still not sure if it's going to last" I replied, much to the delight of everyone there.

So Michael was prepared to take my lead on this one. It certainly sounded like something God had been preparing me for over the years. I felt that it was definitely something I wanted to do. So we went along the usual lines of, if I apply and if I'm offered an interview then I'll go for it, and if I'm interviewed but not offered the job then we know where we stand, likewise if I am offered the job - it was meant to be. It was, apparently, meant to be. So yet again we upped sticks and set off on a new adventure.

It was a very interesting time we had in Cheltenham but sadly it only lasted less than three years. It was discovered that the money that had been allocated for the new post of operations manager had not been sufficient for it to be permanent fixture. Lack of funds meant that one member of the clergy team and one member of the lay staff would be made redundant. Since I was the most expensive it was clearly going to be me.

It was all rather a shock, as we'd imagined my staying in post until retirement. Since we were renting a house that was dependent on my salary, yet again we faced homelessness. Did we have the faith to rely on past experience and trust that since God had called us there, then he would also provide a way of escape and a new future for us? If I'm being honest the answer has to be - not really!

Since Michael was already retirement age, and I was only three years off it, things did look rather serious. Someone suggested that we contact some of the organisations that help supply retirement housing for church workers and missionaries. This we duly did and we found ourselves invited down to Gravesend to meet one such community that had a very small apartment available. Even the name of the town made me feel despondent - neither of us actually felt we were ready for that kind of retirement! Nevertheless we were made very welcome and assured that we would almost certainly be offered accommodation.

Although the sense of relief was palpable we still drove back to Cheltenham feeling very broken and dispirited. We were driving along a country road, a few miles from the nearest town, and talking through our woes. Michael was driving and I was getting more and more overwrought thinking about our future - or lack of one. I remember being in full flight and starting to say "but why do we always end up being broken hearted?" Actually, I only got as far as "but why do we always end up being . . ." I stopped mid-flow because to the left of us was a large empty field, with not a building anywhere in sight. Standing in the field was a large billboard clearly visible from the road. This billboard said just one thing:

Only Jesus Heals the Broken-hearted

I remember thinking "that's it - I've lost it - I'm hallucinating!". I turned to Michael and practically screamed "Did you see that?" He didn't answer me, he didn't need to; I could see the tears streaming down his face.

When we eventually calmed down we knew that deep down peace again "which the world cannot give". Yes, our heavenly Father was going to rescue us again - and yes, we did have a future; but little could we have imagined how quickly he would act on our behalf!

That evening, feeling both shaken and stirred we went to our friend's house for dinner. We had made friends with Jonathan and Martha as soon as we had arrived in Cheltenham and found that we had a lot of shared in interests. To be honest, Jonathan is the only friend I have who shares my passion for fonts - no, not those found in churches but typefaces! At last, a fellow nerd. Not too surprising I suppose that he was working in the IT section of GCHQ based in Cheltenham. Quite a few of his colleagues also attended our church. Indeed, when I had been interviewed for the post I had gone on a walk around the parish to discuss its profile with the Rural Dean. "I suppose it's fair to say" he told me "that the congregation is largely made up of two sorts of people - they're either spies or they're teachers!" Perhaps that why we had fitted in so well there.

Jonathan and Martha wanted to know how our visit to Gravesend went, and quickly picked up on our despondency. About ten minutes into the meal Jonathan suddenly announced that he had something he wanted to tell us. Both he and Martha had had their own houses before they married, now they lived in one and had folk living in the other until recently. "We've decided to sell our spare house here and buy another one for people to rent - we were thinking of a place somewhere like . . . . . oh, Aylesbury for example!" The smiles on their faces and the look of utter amazement on ours must have been in stark contrast. Why had they picked Aylesbury and why did our hearts leap when we heard it? Because our Carolyn and family had been living there since she married and started a family. We had shared with them that Carolyn's marriage was going through increasingly difficult times, and that we so wanted to be there for her.

And so our dear friends bought that house in Aylesbury which we rented for a very modest rate for just over three years; I'm sure they had no idea just how grateful we were. It was perfect timing of course. As Carolyn's marriage came to a slow and painful end we were there for her and the children.

It was a fairly straightforward move to Aylesbury, which since we often went to stay with the family, we knew well, and also felt quite at home at Holy Trinity church, where we had already started to get to know people. I even managed to get a new job before we even moved there. This time I spotted the advert myself! Manchester University was running the education programmes for the Buckingham prison services and was looking for people with Adult Education teaching skills who could teach IT to the inmates. I went for an interview in a hotel somewhere and had to do a teaching session with a few adults who were far more awkward and obstructive than any of the real prisoners I was to teach.

I actually started teaching before we had completed the move and had to do some long-distance commuting for a couple of months. I worked around three days a week sometimes starting before nine in the morning and often doing an evening session finishing around nine. It was certainly one of the most interesting and satisfying jobs I had ever done. I worked mainly in an open prison which held a number of men who had committed 'white collar crimes' and so forth - there were even a couple of MP's! But there were also a number of lifers coming to the end of long sentences and being prepared to return to society.

I found myself teaching website design to people who barely knew what the Internet was, yet if they were going to get work by running their own small business, then it was pretty essential that they learned. I found myself working with three other IT trainers teaching coding and all the Microsoft Qualifications, I was also the graphic and web design specialist. Most weeks I usually also worked a few hours a week in the category B prison next door which housed a number of serious criminals and lifers.

On my induction day, one of the IT team I was to work with came to find me and invited me to join her for a coffee. We chatted generally, slightly beating around the bushes, when she suddenly blurted out "you're a Christian aren't you?" "Yes" I replied, though I wasn't sure that I had indicated that in any way. "Well" she said "this is a very male orientated place to work and as soon as my previous colleague left, who gave me quite a hard time, I started praying that his replacement would be: a women, a Christian and someone with a sense of humour." "Two out of three's not bad" I responded with a dead straight face.

I got on very well with Anne (not her real name) and eventually with the two guys, who happened to be father and son. The father was incredibly misogynistic, and although he knew I was better qualified than any of them, kept insisting that as I would be responsible at times for invigilating the learners taking the Microsoft exams online, then perhaps I ought to sit them myself so that I would know how they worked. We both knew that I really didn't need to do that and at first I declined. Eventually I got so annoyed with his attitude that I sat down one afternoon and did over three hours of continuous tests, going through every level. When the results came back he was rather shocked that I had achieved an average score of 98.5% on all the tests. The average pass rate was 76% and that included both staff and learners. I found it both sad and funny that he treated me with much greater respect after that. His son, who I got on very well with, leaked my results to the men one day, which much improved my street cred. After all, I was as old as some of their mothers, or grandmothers even - so what would I know about IT! What annoyed me most of all though, was the fact that I felt that Microsoft was out of step with the real world at the particular time (they came back into sync with a big jump a year or so later) and I disagreed with a lot of the ways they were teaching people to use IT. So I merely answered the questions in the way I knew would score the point, and not in the way I would be teaching the subject. I felt almost as if I had perjured myself just to prove a point.

One of the safety lectures we received as prison staff was not to reveal any of our personal details to the men. I was not at all phased by the thought that one of them might track me down after they left prison - after all I treated them all with respect and kindness. Anne was of a far more nervous nature however, but she was a kind soul and had assisted the Prison chaplaincy staff with a few sessions of the Alpha courses they ran regularly - and which were the means by which a number of men found a life-changing faith. The open prison system had a fairly fast through-put and Anne had no sooner seen one particular lifer come to faith than he was out of the system and back home.

Anne lived in a village not far from the prisons and went to a local church there. She readily joined in when all the local churches came to together to do their own version of the Oberammergau Passion Play at Easter. Imagine her surprise and concern when she saw the ex-prisoner at the auditions and realised that he now lived in her village. Later she told me that she had great misgiving when she realised that he had been cast in the role of Christ, but she also knew that the selection panel, and clergy etc., would certainly know about his past since all ex-lifers most declare their status in such contexts. She went on to tell me that she stood on the side of the road on that Good Friday with tears streaming down her face as she watched a truly repentant and forgiven man bearing publicly the cross that had set him free.

Two evenings a week, I would spend two to three hours in a large Nissan hut with between twenty and thirty prisoners, some of whom were completing life sentences for murder, all on my own. There was a telephone in the small staff office at one end of the hut, but I usually worked at the other end. I had, however, been supplied with a brown leather belt on which I kept my keys and a whistle which I was to blow in case of emergency. Since the prison officers were usually in a building about a quarter of a mile away I would have had to have blown that whistle very loud and very long to attract attention. But strangely I never once felt afraid in that context; I suspect that was because I was aware that if one of the prisoners had gone for me, the others would have dealt with the situation in no uncertain terms. Indeed, during one daytime class a new student appeared out of nowhere and as I started to introduce him to the curriculum, he became somewhat rude and offensive in his response, which I just did my best to ignore. The men made their own tea and coffee in the kitchen in the teaching block during the breaks. I left them for about ten minutes while I went to get my own coffee and collect my post. When I got back I sensed a slight tension in the air, I also noticed that the new student was somewhat subdued. I had the sense not to ask what had gone on, but I can only say that he was always extremely polite from that time onwards.

Another incident that remains in my memory from my HMP years is that of a Christian guy who had lost his way and ended up embezzling large sums of money from his company. I taught him for a couple of years and got to know him quite well. I picked up that he was dreading going back home to face up to friends and family, and more especially his church fellowship - would they welcome him back? As the time for his release approached he seemed more and more anxious.

Every morning during the forty-minute drive to work I would pray by name for each of the men I would be working with that day. Most of them I knew little if anything of their back stories, but some I knew quite well. One particular morning there had been heavy snow and it was a long slow drive. Alan (not his real name) kept coming to mind and I kept praying that God would relieve his anxiety. When I finally arrived at work I discovered that Alan wouldn't be in class that day as he was working in a charity shop in Oxford, this was part of his preparation for leaving the system. When I went over to the office at break time to collect my mail I popped a little card into his pigeonhole. On it I had written a verse that had come to mind as I had been praying for him that morning:

For I know the plans I have for you, declares the Lord, plans to prosper you and not to harm you, plans to give you hope and a future. (Jeremiah 29:11)

I know these verses were first spoken by God to the nation of Israel, and I have heard learned folk say this means they are not for the individual, but I disagree. I know God often spoke of the nation of Israel as if they were an individual, he called them his beloved. God speaks to me as the individual I am, and I know I am his beloved. He had plans for Israel and he has plans for me - all good. I can't see the difference, and feel that this is a significant statement, full of promise for all who accept it. Well, despite his failings, Alan had accepted it, but was depressed and scared and greatly in need of encouragement. So I scrawled the verse on a little card, popped it in an envelope and left it for him to find when he returned that evening. Apparently I had forgotten to sign it.

An hour or so later I was surprised to find the men who were supposed to be out working coming back into the classroom, apparently the minibus couldn't make it through the snow, so I sent them off with the others to have their coffee break. A few minutes later Alan literally burst into the empty room waving a piece of card saying "did you write this?" "Yes" I said, cautiously. He promptly collapsed onto a chair and broke down in front of me. When he had recovered he told me that he had been awake in the early hours worrying and getting more and more anxious about the future, and was even starting to feel suicidal. When he got up he, very despondently, did his daily Bible reading - and guess what - it included that verse from Jeremiah that I was to write down for him later that day! He wanted to believe that God had good plans for him, but it was all getting so hard for him to actually trust that. So he turned to God in despair over his lack of faith praying something along the lines of "if this verse is true, and if it's meant for me, then please, somehow, have it repeated for me sometime today." Well how likely was that in his current context? And yet it happened!

We don't have to be mighty prayer warriors to see our prayers answered, just willing to pray as instructed sometimes; and we don't have to be great men and women of faith to believe that God will comfort us in times of need, just willing to be brave and humble and ask for confirmation in the way Alan did. A few weeks later, I was waving him goodbye, a different man from the one I had worried over a few weeks before. He was now smiling and confident with an inner yet visible peace. All kinds of quite unexpected things had opened up for him as he completed his sentence and he was now ready to take on the challenge. I trust that God has continued to bless Alan. Much as I enjoyed that work - changes were afoot. And although we were very content and grateful in our little house in Aylesbury, I often looked out of the window at other houses and sometimes in my heart yearned for a 'permanent home with a view'. Each time that happened I felt comforted, as if God was saying, 'just be patient, there's more to come'. When I told Michael this once, he said 'oh, so you're waiting for a cottage with roses round the door are you?' 'Yes, I replied, and also with a view!' All I got back was a wry grin.

From Aylesbury to the Highlands

We had, as we had hoped, been around to help Carolyn and the children at a very difficult time. She and her husband had now separated, and divorce proceedings had started. Meanwhile our Simon and his lovely wife Belinda were living in Alsager in Cheshire, close to Belinda's parents. Bel was working as a school administrator and Simon was teaching outdoor pursuits at an agricultural college. Belinda's mother had, sadly, died of cancer a few years before, but wonderfully came to faith in her last months. So Bel had been helping her dad out, as well as working, and also finding herself expecting their first child. Her father did not get to see much of his only grandchild as he died two years after Merry was born.

Now feeling that there wasn't anything to keep them in that part of the world they started looking for somewhere to live in Fort William in the Highlands of Scotland. It was a place they were familiar with, since they were both heavily into outdoor pursuits, and often visited for both skiing and climbing. They knew it was likely that Simon would get a job teaching at the Highlands and Islands University based in Fort William, which indeed he did, and felt that it would be a lovely place to bring up their son. We were in Alsager with them one weekend looking after Merry while they finished clearing Bel's parent's house. I had been telling them how the decision had recently been made to greatly reduce the number of subjects offered in the prison education service, and so, yet again, I was about to be made redundant. They then started telling us about their plans to move to Scotland. We had once popped over the border to attend a conference in Scotland, but that was actually all we had seen of the place. So when, out of the blue, the question was asked, how would we feel about joining them in a new adventure, we both paused for at least three seconds before both responding in the affirmative! It was something that had never entered our thinking, and yet it just felt so right. One of the many reasons for them wanting to move to the Highlands was that house prices were, at that time, considerably lower than elsewhere. Such a move would mean they could live in a setting they loved and afford to buy housing for all of us.

This exciting turn of events did have an immediate downside to it of course - we now had to tell Carolyn that we were leaving Aylesbury, which felt quite heartbreaking as she was going through such a difficult time and it felt like we were abandoning her! The Saturday after we got back from Cheshire she and I were attending a conference together, about an hour's drive away, and I knew that I would have to tell her our news sometime during the day. We started off by leaving late, Carolyn was driving and I was learning to use the satnav on my phone, only I keyed in the wrong postcode and we set off completely in the wrong direction. I would never have spotted the mistake and we would probably still be driving now, but fortunately Carolyn is like her father and carries a map book in her head. We go lost a couple more times, thanks to me, before we finally arrived, somewhat fraught and an hour late. We headed for what seemed like the front door of the hall, but when we opened it, it was jam packed with seats and nowhere for us to fit in. So we went round the back of the building to find another way in. Having found ourselves in a broom cupboard and been overcome by a fit of giggles, we opened another door, only to find ourselves standing practically next to the speaker and gazing at a somewhat bemused audience. We backed out and waited for the coffee break before we tried again. At lunch time I found myself wandering around looking at book displays whilst Carolyn was networking. All I could think about was telling Carolyn about the planned move, and how hurt she would be. In desperation I was almost praying out loud for help.

My mind went back to that day when as a teenager I had sat in Holy Trinity Church during Holiday Club asking for guidance on the 'Michael' question. God had spoken to me clearly then, and many times since, but I also knew that I was too old to still be playing Bible lottery. But I was desperate, should we actually be considering going to Scotland, and if so how was I to tell her? I saw a display of books for sale on a windowsill - I just picked one up saying 'please Lord, just show me'. Well it wasn't a Bible, but what I really wanted was just that, comfort and affirmation from scripture, nothing else would really do. I flipped it open and plonked my finger on a page. The book was by Joyce Huggett, and was called *Open to God*. My finger landed, not on her words but on a verse from scripture that she was quoting - Acts 10:20 to be precise. Before my eyes were the words *Do not hesitate to go with them, for I have sent them*. Somehow the burden lifted and I told Carolyn just before we started the drive home; we laughed and cried our way home, and she was gracious enough to remind me that since we had been around for her children, it was only right that we were there also there for Simon's family.

That verse from Acts was not just a comfort to Michael and me, but also for Simon and Belinda, since this was a big move forward for them and they needed to know that they were heading in the direction God had planned. As it happened, shortly after we had arrived in Fort William, Carolyn was appointed as a lecturer in theology at the Methodist college in Yorkshire, not far from Sheffield. By this stage Bethany and Holly were independent, so she and Gideon, who was in his last two years of school, moved to a house in the grounds of the college and started a new life. So had we stayed in Aylesbury it would have felt rather odd. Yet again, despite our doubts and fear, everything came together in the right way at just the right time. That verse that we were given in our early days together still stood: *first prepare your work in the field and then build your house.*

Well the house turned out to be a lovely three-bedroom house by the side of Loch Linnhe on the edge of Fort William. We have a spare room for visitors, and it's been great having family and old friends coming to stay; I have a study where I look out over the loch and watch local boats, yachts and the occasional cruise ship go by, and Michael has a large attic in which he constructs, deconstructs, and then reconstructs some wonderful vintage model railway layouts. And oh yes, I nearly forget, there are indeed roses growing round the door!

We've been In Fort William nearly ten years now and still enjoy life, albeit at a slower pace. The Sjögren's Syndrome does not improve with age and when I'm out I mostly use a walker or wheelchair, but it doesn't stop us travelling. Indeed, about two weeks after returning from yet another trip to America, to visit the Four Corners and the Grand Canyon, the whole Scottish adventure was just starting and we drove up to Fort William to start looking for a house. As I said, we had barely crept over the border before, but now we did that long drive from Glasgow along the side of Loch Lomond and then across Rannoch Moor. I knew Scotland had a reputation of being a beautiful country, but I had no idea just how beautiful. Time after time on that journey we found ourselves driving through world-class scenery, only to round a bend in the road and be greeted by another breath-taking view. No matter how many time we make that journey I don't think I shall ever tire of it.

We are privileged to watch the family story continue with our children and grandchildren. Carolyn went on to become the Youth and Children's Advisor for the Diocese of York, and is now the National Youth and Children's Officer for the Church of England. She married the wonderful Melvyn and together they enjoy working on their home, ministry and dog.

Simon continues to climb mountains and take Merry and Rose for overnight camps in the wild, canoeing and sailing, not to mention canyoning and cycling. In his spare time he runs a very successful First Aid training business. The family attend the local Free Church, which we also attended for four years, I even worked part-time as their administrator. We left simply because as a denomination they seemed to not even be thinking about including women in any leadership roles, we're not talking ordination here, just that they do not have a single designated role for a woman, she's not even able to be an elder. We had assumed in our early days with them that they would be slowly moving forward (everything moves slowly in the Highlands of Scotland) but when we found absolutely no evidence of that we felt we couldn't stay, much as we loved that church family. Somewhat to our amazement we are now happily part of a non-denominational church fellowship called

The Mustard Seed. It feels like a real family and is just as chaotic as a real family! I still yearn for a good cathedral service now and then, and regularly watch *Songs of Praise* for a hymn fix; but all in all I know we're in the right place. Michael and I are both on the preaching and leading rota, and I also help out with the *Thought for the Day* now and then for the local radio station.

So we have family on the other side of town who are always dropping by, and we often pop over to see them and their flocks of chickens and ducks, looked after by our lovely daughter-in-law Bel! We have friends at church and I now have a new batch of lovely friends I've made at the local craft club I run each Friday in town, which means that I have plenty of happy things going on in my life. I have finally gotten around to passing on my website design business, which will give me more time for my hobbies - I certainly don't intend getting bored. Recently someone asked if I would consider taking on the role of fairy Godmother for the local pantomime - just the thought of that brought a twinkle to my eye!

So the story of the poor little duck who started by having her wings clipped draws to a close. She grew new wings and learned how to soar and enjoy God's world. She met the love of her life when not much more than a child, and found a kind, funny and wonderful partner to fly through life with her. With him she learned that their Heavenly Father does indeed keep his promises, and that no matter how many times they failed him, not once did he ever fail them. Indeed, they saw and experienced his provision in ways which they still find amazing. The little duck grew up - still just a duck - but tall in the water.

Appendix – Report From Barnardo's

(composed 2002)

BACKGROUND HISTORY

LESLEY WELLS previously DOROTHY ROSEMARY PETERS birth name DOROTHY ROSANNA MAGEE

This history was prepared from information given at the time leading up to and including the adoption and held on microfilm

Lesley was born at West Ham in East London on 11th of April 1950. She was named Dorothy Rosanna Magee by her parents Hilda Lillian Dorothy Magee and James Robert Leonards Magee. The family then lived in Plaistow East London

Hilda was born in Forest Gate and James was from Ireland. Hilda had remained at home keeping house for her father after her mother's death in 1943. She later met James and they were married in September 1946. Their first child, Leonard, was born on 17th August 1947

James had been a corporal in the army but later developed T.B. and died in December 1950. By this time Hilda was expecting their third child, also James, who was born on 11th March 1951

In about 1950 Hilda and James had moved to 2 Roding Streed, Forest Gate, this being quite a large house which Hilda looked after well.

When interviewed Hilda stated that the marriage was not very happy but she later took care of James during his illness.

After James' death Hilda took work as a presser but she found she was unable to cope with working, taking the children to and from day nursery and running the house. Hilda became nervous and irritable but was unable to take up the treatment that was offered as she could not make arrangements for the children.

As time went by Hilda's condition deteriorated and in December 1952 she asked Barnardo's to take care of Lesley. Apparently although Hilda was thought to look after Lesley as well as the two boys she stated that she did not feel as close to her as she did to Leonard and James. This she believes was because James had ill-treated her during the period that she was expecting Lesley and at that time she resented her.

After assessing the circumstances Barnardo's agreed to admit Lesley to care and on 23rd February 1953 she went to live at St. Christopher's, a Barnardo's residential nursery in Tunbridge Wells, Kent.

Lesley was medically examined on a mission and no health problems were apparent. She was then described as a "friendly and quite child".

However, Hilda's health did not improve and she was due to be admitted to a psychiatric unit at St. Georges hospital in Hornchurch, Essex. The local children's department asked Barnardo's to admit Leonard and James on a temporary basis until Hilda could resume their care. Therefore on 10th March 1953 the boys joined Lesley at St. Christopher's. The doctors at the hospital thought that Hilda would need treatment for about a three month period.

Leonard and James were returned to Hilda on 1st July 1953 but by December 1953 Lesley was still in care. It was agreed that Lesley should be placed in a foster home and on 24th of October 1953 she went to live with Muriel and Thomas Peters in Redhill, Surrey. Hilda was informed of this. Apparently Lesley was happy in this home and progressed well. It would seem that there was some contact between Hilda and the foster parents mainly by letter but she did also visit. When Lesley had lived with them for over 2 years she gave agreement to the couple adopting Lesley.

Hilda was seen towards the end of February 1956 when she signed the initial form of agreement to adoption having had the meaning of this fully explained to her.

Hilda was thought to present as "rather tense" and her home was "extremely clean and well furnished". She had been working as a machinist but was going to leave as she did not like the work. She talked of visiting James at St. Christopher's and hoped that he would move nearer to her. Leonard by now was in Australia.

Hilda was once more pregnant and was anxious about making arrangements for the care of the baby as she once more felt unable to cope on her own. Reports in March and June 1956 stated that Lesley appeared "very happy" and that Muriel and Thomas were keen for the adoption to go ahead. They indicated that they would not object to contact being kept with James if he was fostered near to them, but they were unsure how much future involvement with Hilda would be appropriate. They had, however, promised to send her a photo of Lesley which Barnardo's advised should be after the adoption was finalised.

At this point Lesley was described as "a delightful little girl, very friendly, has a dog and a cat of whom she is very fond. Has just started ballet dancing, loves painting, helping with the housework. Is an extremely active child, easy to manage, so interested in everything and obviously very happy and secure".

In May 1956 Barnardo's gave formal agreement to Muriel and Thomas making an application to adopt Lesley. Arrangements were then made for Hilda to sign the legal consent form for Lesley's adoption.

Hilda was seen again in July 1956. The baby was due in the August and although Hilda had collected necessary items to look after the baby early on she was still seeking alternatives for the baby's long term care. Hilda talked once more of visiting James and the possibility of him moving to the village homes in Barkingside was discussed so that he would be nearer to her. This took place in October 1956. Hilda was aware that Lesley's adoption would shortly be taking place. An adoption order was granted on 18th September 1956 at Reigate county court. Apparently some contact continued between the family and Hilda. She sent letters and the occasional present. The parents were aware that Hilda was later talking of going to Australia, possibly taking James with her. He eventually had returned to live with Hilda in September 1958. Muriel and Thomas stated that they would have no objection if Lesley later wanted to meet her mother.

Printed in Great Britain
by Amazon

39629546R00158